Chapter 1: Poverty in the UK

Chapter 2: Global Poverty

Introduction

The Poverty Crisis is Volume 235 in the *Issues* series. The aim of the series is to offer current, diverse information about important issues in our world, from a UK perspective.

ABOUT THE POVERTY CRISIS

Poverty is characterised by the severe deprivation of basic human needs such as food, housing, safe drinking water, health and education. In the year 2000, the UN's Millenium Development Goals declared the aim of eradicating extreme poverty and hunger by 2015. Although progress has been made, there are still billions of people in the developing world surviving on less than £0.80 a day. Shockingly, poverty is also a crippling issue for the UK, with 13 million people currently living on 60% or less of the average household income. This book investigates poverty on a global and a local scale and examines ways in which we can tackle this crisis.

OUR SOURCES

Titles in the *Issues* series are designed to function as educational resource books, providing a balanced overview of a specific subject.

The information in our books is comprised of facts, articles and opinions from many different sources, including:

- Newspaper reports and opinion pieces
- Website fact sheets
- Magazine and journal articles
- Statistics and surveys
- Government reports
- Literature from special interest groups

A NOTE ON CRITICAL EVALUATION

Because the information reprinted here is from a number of different sources, readers should bear in mind the origin of the text and whether the source is likely to have a particular bias when presenting information (or when conducting their research). It is hoped that, as you read about the many aspects of the issues explored in this book, you will critically evaluate the information presented.

It is important that you decide whether you are being presented with facts or opinions. Does the writer give a biased or unbiased report? If an opinion is being expressed, do you agree with the writer? Is there potential bias to the 'facts' or statistics behind an article?

ASSIGNMENTS

In the back of this book, you will find a selection of assignments designed to help you engage with the articles you have been reading and to explore your own opinions. Some tasks will take longer than others and there is a mixture of design, writing and research based activities that you can complete alone or in a group.

FURTHER RESEARCH

At the end of each article we have listed its source and a website that you can visit if you would like to conduct your own research. Please remember to critically evaluate any sources that you consult and consider whether the information you are viewing is accurate and unbiased.

The Poverty Crisis

Series Editor: Cara Acred

Volume 235

Independence Educational Publishers

First published by Independence Educational Publishers

The Studio, High Green

Great Shelford

Cambridge CB22 5EG

England

© Independence 2012

Copyright

Photocopy licence

British Library Cataloguing in Publication Data

The poverty crisis. – (Issues ; v. 235)

1. Poverty. 2. Poverty – Great Britain. 3. Poverty – Prevention. 4. Poverty – Great Britain – Prevention.

I. Series II. Acred, Cara.

362.5-dc23

ISBN-13: 9781 86168 628 2

Printed in Great Britain

MWL Print Group Ltd

What is poverty?

Definitions of poverty really matter. They set the standards by which we determine whether the incomes and living conditions of the poorest in society are acceptable or not. From this follow all actions to help the poorest.

Absolute and overall poverty

Absolute poverty has been seen as a matter of acute deprivation, hunger, premature death and suffering. This captures an important understanding of poverty and its relevance remains widespread in parts of the world today. It focuses attention on the urgent need for action.

However, while there are some circumstances, such as starvation or unsafe water, which do lead to immediate death, most of these criteria require judgements and comparisons. What is classed as acute deprivation will vary from society to society and through time, and what is counted as premature death will depend on average life expectancies. So while there is a core to ideas of absolute poverty relating to the severity of deprivation and the need for immediate action, in practice, it is part of a continuum of a measurement of poverty, indicating it is deeper and worse.

As such, in 1995 the United Nations adopted two definitions of poverty.

Absolute poverty was defined as:

A condition characterised by severe deprivation of basic human needs, including food, safe drinking water, sanitation facilities, health, shelter, education and information. It depends not only on income but also on access to services.

Overall poverty takes various forms, including:

⇨ Lack of income and productive resources to ensure sustainable livelihoods;

⇨ hunger and malnutrition;

⇨ ill health;

⇨ limited or lack of access to education and other basic services;

⇨ increased morbidity and mortality from illness;

⇨ homelessness and inadequate housing;

⇨ unsafe environments and social discrimination and exclusion.

It is also characterised by lack of participation in decision making and in civil, social and cultural life. It occurs in all countries:

⇨ as mass poverty in many developing countries,

⇨ pockets of poverty amid wealth in developed countries,

⇨ loss of livelihoods as a result of economic recession,

⇨ sudden poverty as a result of disaster or conflict,

⇨ the poverty of low-wage workers,

⇨ and the utter destitution of people who fall outside family support systems, social institutions and safety nets.

(UN, 1995)

These are relative definitions of poverty, which see poverty in terms of minimum acceptable standards of living within the society in which a particular person lives.

Millennium Development Goals

In 2000, world leaders came together at United Nations Headquarters in New York to adopt the United Nations Millennium Declaration. This declaration committed their nations to a new global partnership to reduce extreme poverty and set out a series of time-bound targets – with a deadline of 2015 – that have become known as the Millennium Development Goals.

The development goals cover eight areas:

⇨ End poverty and hunger

⇨ Universal education

⇨ Gender equality

⇨ Child health

⇨ Maternal health

⇨ Combat HIV/AIDS

⇨ E n v i r o n m e n t a l sustainability

⇨ Global partnership.

The goal of eradicating extreme poverty and hunger sets three targets to be reached by 2015. Using 1990 as the base, it aims to:

⇨ halve the proportion of people whose income is less than $1 a day;

⇨ achieve full and productive employment and decent work for all, including women and young people;

⇨ halve the proportion of people who suffer from hunger.

In 2010, the United Nations reported on progress towards these targets in *The Millennium Development Goals Report.* Detailed data on progress towards meeting these targets can be found on the UN's Millennium Development Goals Indicators website.

Setting a poverty reduction target has undoubtedly raised awareness of world poverty and directed action towards this goal. However, setting the target at halving the proportion of people living on less than $1 a day can be criticised, as with other income-based measures, as being arbitrary and the level of $1 a day limiting.

⇨ Information from PSE2011. Please visit www.pse2011. com for more information on this and other subjects.

Relative poverty, absolute poverty and social exclusion

Information from The Poverty Site.

Poverty versus social exclusion

Prior to the 1997 Labour Government, the term 'social exclusion' was rarely, if ever, used when discussing social policy in the UK. Rather, the word 'poverty' was generally used as an all-encompassing term to describe situations where people lack many of the opportunities that are available to the average citizen. Whilst low income was central to this notion, it also covered other factors relating to severe and chronic disadvantage.

However, some people used the word 'poverty' in the narrower sense of simply low income. It was to ensure that the wider notion – that disadvantage can cover a wider range of factors than 'just' low income – was not lost, that the Government started using the term 'social exclusion'.

In other words: the wider notion of 'poverty' = the narrower notion + 'social exclusion'.

One of the advantages of the term 'social exclusion' is that it is reasonably self-explanatory, clearly relating to the alienation or disenfranchisement of certain people within society. Its use therefore helpfully highlights the importance of such alienation and the need to understand the full complexities of its causes and effects.

However, one of the consequences of introducing the term 'social exclusion' was that it led some people to assume that low income and alienation were essentially unconnected and that each could (and should) be considered separately when developing policy. This, in turn, led to the tendency in some circles to downgrade the importance of addressing issues of low income, on the grounds that its effect was simply to limit the material goods that a

household could acquire rather than having any wider social impact.

In reaction to all this, The Poverty Site generally uses the term 'poverty and social exclusion' throughout, without differentiating between them. This usage has several advantages, namely:

It emphasises that the issue of concern is both low income and the other factors relating to severe and chronic disadvantage, and that these are closely connected.

Its overall scope is the same whether the word 'poverty' is used in its wide or narrow sense.

Relative versus absolute poverty

For the sake of simplicity, the discussion below relates to income poverty only (i.e. the narrow sense of the word 'poverty' above). It would, however, equally apply to the wider notion.

Absolute poverty refers to a set standard which is the same in all countries and which does not change over time. An income-related example would be living on less than $X per day.

Relative poverty refers to a standard which is defined in terms of the society in which an individual lives and which therefore differs between countries and over time. An income-related example would be living on less than X% of average UK income.

Absolute poverty and relative poverty are both valid concepts. The concept of absolute poverty is that there are minimum standards below which no one anywhere in the world should ever fall. The concept of relative poverty is that, in a rich country such as the UK, there are higher minimum standards below which no one should fall, and that these standards should rise if and as the country becomes richer.

Absolute poverty

Clearly, where both absolute and relative poverty are prevalent, it is absolute poverty which is (by far) the more serious issue. This is the case in much of the third world, where the focus is therefore on fixed income thresholds (typically $1 or $2 a day, on the grounds that this is the minimum needed for mere survival). But in a UK setting, such thresholds have no import: no one in the UK lives on incomes anywhere near this low.

So, logically, either one concludes that there is no absolute poverty in the UK or that a much higher threshold of absolute poverty than $1 or $2 per day should be used.

The view that there is no absolute poverty in the UK is a perfectly valid position to take.

The view that there should be an absolute poverty threshold but that it should be much higher than $1 or $2 per day begs the question about how such a threshold should be defined and on what basis.

In the UK, the main efforts to define such thresholds have been undertaken under the general heading of 'minimum income standards', which basically estimate the level of income required to purchase a given basket of goods and services. But the key point about such initiatives is that the basket of goods and services is defined according to the norms of the day and, as such, are inherently relative rather than absolute in nature. So, for example, there would be many items in the 'today's basket' that would not have been in the basket 50 years ago. In other words, 'minimum income standards' relate to relative poverty rather than to absolute poverty.

In recent years, the Government has begun to describe households with less than half[1] the average 1997 household income (after adjusting for inflation) as being in 'absolute poverty'. This is, however, purely a political device – the only relevance of 1997 is that it is when the current Government came into power.[2] That is not to say that the statistic is unimportant, simply that it should not be described as 'absolute poverty'.

To summarise: there is no obvious way of defining an absolute poverty threshold except the $1 or $2 a day thresholds defined on the grounds that this is the minimum needed for mere survival. But in a UK setting, such thresholds have no import: no one in the UK lives on incomes anywhere near this low.

Relative poverty

The view that relative poverty is not important is a perfectly valid position to take – it is just not the view that the authors of this article, along with most other researchers, the EU, the UK Government, and politicians of all hues across the political spectrum take. So, for example, the Government's target of halving child poverty by 2010 was defined in terms of relative poverty.

The reason that we believe that relative poverty is important is because we believe that no one should live with 'resources that are so seriously below those commanded by the average individual or family that they are, in effect, excluded from ordinary living patterns, customs and activities.'[3] In other words, we believe that, in a rich country such as the UK, there should be certain minimum standards below which no one should fall.[4] And, as society becomes richer, so norms change and the levels of income and resources that are considered to be adequate rise. Unless the poorest can keep up with growth in average incomes, they will progressively become more excluded from the opportunities that the rest of society enjoys. If substantial numbers of people do fall below such minimum standards then, not only are they excluded from ordinary living patterns, but it demeans the rest of us and reduces overall social cohesion in our society. It is also needless.

If one accepts that relative poverty is important in principle, then the obvious issue arises of what thresholds to use and on what basis. Our basic answer is that it does not matter, so long as the thresholds are defined in relation to contemporary average (median) income and are for households rather than individuals. It is for this reason that the main indicators on this website use a variety of thresholds, so that a fuller picture of trends can be developed. But, for reasons of consistency and clarity, there has to be a 'headline' threshold

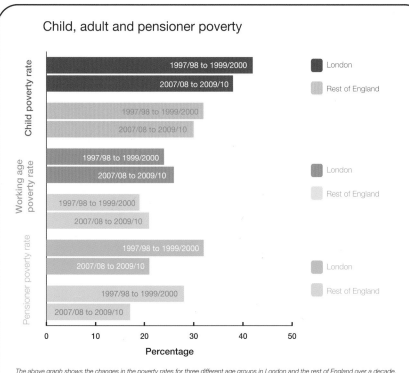

Child, adult and pensioner poverty

The above graph shows the changes in the poverty rates for three different age groups in London and the rest of England over a decade. The poverty rates here are calculated after housing costs (AHC) have been deducted from income.

For all age groups, poverty in London is higher than in the rest of England. The gap is greatest for children: 37% or 590,000 children live in low-income households in London, compared to 28% elsewhere. Though the child poverty rate in London fell in the last ten years, by about 4 percentage points, it is still higher than any other English region.

Pensioner poverty has also come down, both in Inner and Outer London and elsewhere. Overall, 20% or 200,000 pensioners in London live in low-income households, down by a third compared to the rate a decade earlier. The pensioner poverty rate in the rest of England almost halved from 27% to 14% over the same period. By contrast, working-age poverty has risen throughout the country. Overall around 28% or 1.36 million working-age adults in London are in poverty, up from 23% ten years ago. This compares to a rate of 21% in the rest of the country, up from 19% over the decade.

Source: Child adult and pensioner poverty. 11 July 2012. London's poverty profile.
© 2010-11 Trust for London and New Policy Institute

and, for this, we use the same threshold as both the UK Government and the EU, namely a household income of less than 60% of contemporary median household income.

Some people criticise the concept of relative poverty on the grounds that it is to do with 'inequality' rather than 'poverty'. At one level, this is simply an issue of semantics – because of the potential confusion between 'absolute poverty in the third world' and 'relative poverty in the UK', we are also not very comfortable with the phrase 'relative poverty' and this is why we use the more descriptive 'in low-income households' throughout The Poverty Site.

But at another level, the criticism is simply confused: whilst 'inequality' is about differences in income across the whole of the income distribution, 'relative poverty' is about the number of people who have incomes a long way below those of people in the middle of the income distribution. These two things are very different. For example, whilst there will inevitably always be inequality, there is no logical or arithmetical reason why there should always be people in relative poverty.

To summarise: whether one believes that relative poverty is important or not is a matter of opinion, but all political parties in the UK believe that it is important and so do we. There are well-established ways of measuring the extent of relative poverty and it is these methods to which The Poverty Site adheres.

Notes

1. More precisely, less than 60% of median, which is a similar amount of money.

2. Indeed, we once heard a government minister argue that the poverty threshold should be fixed at the beginning of each term of office and then suddenly jump at the start of the next term of office before being fixed again. In that way, every government could say that it was reducing poverty even though levels of poverty never actually fell!

3. The definition of relative poverty as articulated by Professor Peter Townsend, the leading authority of the last 50 years on UK poverty.

4. Webster's dictionary definition of the word 'poverty' is 'the state of one who lacks a usual or socially acceptable amount of money or material possessions'.

⇨ Information from The Poverty Site. Visit www.poverty.org.uk for further information.

© Guy Palmer

UK poverty levels forecast to rise – over 2.5 million more in poverty by 2020

New research warns that the number of (childless) adults of working-age in poverty is predicted to rise by over 40% by 2020.

It also shows that the 2020 child poverty targets will be missed and the number of children in poverty will increase unless drastic action is taken now.

Commissioned by the Joseph Rowntree Foundation, *Child and working-age poverty from 2010 to 2020* is a report by the Institute for Fiscal Studies. It shows the likely impact of tax and benefit policy, alongside economic and demographic change, on child and working-age adult poverty up to 2020.

Julia Unwin, Chief Executive of the Joseph Rowntree Foundation, said:

'This really is bleak news for people who are already struggling. The forecast is for a huge increase in the number of people living below the relative poverty line by 2020. The number of working-age childless adults in poverty is set to rise by over 40% from its current level of 3.4 million to 4.9 million by 2020.

'The research also recognises that the Government's target of reducing child poverty to 10% by 2020 will not be reached. This report forecasts levels of 24% by 2020 on the basis of current policies and anticipated future economic conditions, unless there is radical change both in the economy and in the direction of policy on poverty, governments will continue to fall short of their own targets.

'Overall, this report provides worrying evidence that people and places in poverty are bearing the brunt of government spending cuts. Government cannot ignore this evidence – it must look at how policy can help prevent the forecast increase in poverty levels.

'JRF is committed to monitoring the impact of austerity on people and places in poverty, to help ensure that they do not pay a disproportionate price for the deficit.'

11 October 2011

⇨ Information from the Joseph Rowntree Foundation. Please visit www.jrf.org.uk for further information.

© Joseph Rowntree Foundation

Key facts about poverty

Information from The Poverty Site.

Income

⇨ The most commonly used threshold of low income is a household income that is 60% or less of the average (median) British household income in that year. The latest year for which household income data is available is 2008/09. In that year, the 60% threshold was worth: £119 per week for a single adult with no dependent children; £206 per week for a couple with no dependent children; £202 per week for a single adult with two dependent children under 14; and £288 per week for a couple with two dependent children under 14. These sums of money are measured after income tax, council tax and housing costs have been deducted, where housing costs include rents, mortgage interest (but not the repayment of principal), buildings insurance and water charges. They therefore represent what the household has available to spend on everything else it needs, from food and heating to travel and entertainment.

⇨ In 2008/09, 13 million people in the UK were living in households below this low-income threshold. This is around a fifth (22%) of the population.

⇨ This 13 million figure is an increase of one million compared with four years previously, 2004/05. The increases over the last four years follow six uninterrupted years of decreases from 1998/99 to 2004/05 and are the first increases since 1996/97.

⇨ The number of people on low incomes is still lower (just) than it was during the early 1990s but is much greater than in the early 1980s.

⇨ The proportions of children and pensioners who are in low-income households are both lower than a decade ago. In contrast, the proportion for working-age adults without dependent children is a little higher. A third of all people in low-income households are now working-age adults without dependent children, and the majority of these are single adults rather than couples.

⇨ Around a third of all disabled adults aged 25 to retirement are living in low-income households. This is twice the rate of that for non-disabled adults. The main reason why so many disabled people are in low-income households is their high levels of worklessness. A graduate with a work-limiting disability is more likely to be lacking but wanting work than an unqualified person with no disability.

⇨ Among working-age adults in low income, more than half now live in families where someone is in paid work.

⇨ The level of Income Support for both pensioners and families with two or more children has gone up faster than average earnings since the late 1990s, but that for working-age adults without children has fallen considerably behind.

⇨ Half of all people in social housing are in low-income households compared to one in seven of those in other housing tenures.

⇨ Inner London is deeply divided: it has by far the highest proportion of people in low income but also a high proportion of people on a high income.

⇨ Over the last decade, the poorest tenth of the population have, on average, seen a fall in their real incomes after deducting housing costs. This is in sharp contrast with the rest of the income distribution, which, on average, has seen substantial rises in their real incomes. The richest tenth of the population have seen much bigger proportional rises in their incomes than any other group.

⇨ More than half of all low-income households are paying full Council Tax, noticeably higher than in the mid-1990s.

⇨ The UK has a higher proportion of its population in relative low income than most other EU countries: of the 27 EU countries, only four have a higher rate than the UK. The proportion of people living in relative low income in the UK is twice that of The Netherlands and one-and-a-half times that of France.

> **'In 2008/09, 13 million people in the UK were living in households below this low-income threshold'**

Child poverty

⇨ The number of children living in low-income households was 3.9 million in 2008/09 (measuring income after deducting housing costs). The Government's short term child poverty target was to reduce the number of children in low-income households by a quarter by 2004/05 compared with 1998/99. This implied a maximum of 3.3 million children living in low-income households by 2004/05. Given that the actual number in 2008/09 was 3.9 million, the Government is still 0.6 million above its 2004/05 target.

⇨ A half of all lone parents are in low income, more than twice the rate for couples with children.

⇨ More than half of all the children in low-income households have someone in their family doing paid work.

⇨ Although the number of children who are in workless households is somewhat lower than a decade ago, the UK still has a higher proportion than any other EU country.

Older people

⇨ Until the last few years, the proportion of pensioners living in low-income households had been falling sharply, from 29% of all pensioners in 1997/98 to 17% in 2005/06. There has, however, been no significant reduction since 2005/06. Pensioners now account for just one sixth of all the people in low-income households.

⇨ A third of all pensioner households entitled to Pension Credit are not claiming it.

⇨ The proportion of people aged 75 and over who receive home care to help them live at home has almost halved since the mid-1990s. County councils and unitary authorities support far fewer households than either urban or Welsh authorities.

Work

⇨ In 2010, there were 4.7 million people of working age who wanted to be in paid work but were not. The number has been rising since 2005, when it stood at 3.4 million. Only half of these people are officially unemployed, with the others being considered to be 'economically inactive', either because they are able to start work immediately or because they are not actively seeking work. Lone parents and those who are sick or disabled usually count as 'economically inactive' rather than 'unemployed'.

'5% of people live in overcrowded conditions'

⇨ Until 2008, the number of people claiming out-of-work benefits had been falling steadily. Between February 2008 and February 2010, however, numbers rose sharply, back to the levels of a decade previously. All of this rise was in the number of unemployed claimants, which, by February 2010, was actually substantially higher than a decade previously. The number of sick or disabled claimants remained unchanged.

⇨ One in four adults with a work-limiting disability are not working but want to. This compares with one in 15 of those with no work-limiting disability. At all levels of qualification, the proportion of people with a work-limiting disability who lack but want paid work is much greater than for those without a work-limiting disability.

'One in ten 16- to 18-year-olds are not in education, employment or training'

⇨ In 2010, the unemployment rate among young adults aged 16 to 24 was 25%. This proportion has been rising since 2004, when it was 12%.

⇨ Throughout most of the last decade, around two-fifths of those losing their job had had that job for less than six months. Only a quarter of temporary employees do not want a permanent job.

⇨ People without qualifications are three times less likely to receive job-related training compared with those with some qualifications.

Low pay

⇨ Around three million adults aged 22 to retirement were paid less than £7 per hour in 2010. Two-thirds of these were women and more than half were part-time workers.

⇨ The proportion of workers aged 22 and over who were low paid fell between 2002 and 2005 but has remained broadly unchanged since then.

⇨ Though still substantial, the pay gap between low-paid men and low-paid women is less than a decade ago.

⇨ A quarter of workers earning less than £7 per hour work in the public sector.

⇨ The lower a person's qualifications, the more likely they are to be low paid. For example, half of employees aged 25 to 29 with no GCSEs at grade C or above were paid less than £7 per hour in 2009 compared to one in ten of those with degrees or equivalent. All levels of qualifications appear to make a noticeable difference compared with the level below.

⇨ In 2010, just one in nine employees earning £7 an hour or less belonged to a trade union, a much smaller proportion than for those with higher hourly earnings.

⇨ One in six working-age households are now in receipt of tax credits over and above the (non-means tested) family element. In total, three times as many households are now in receipt of tax credits compared with a decade ago.

Education

⇨ 11-year-olds: over the last decade, the proportion of 11-year-olds not reaching level 4 at Key Stage 2 has fallen from 25% to 19% for English, and from 28% to 20% in Maths. These proportions are also falling for schools with a high number of children from deprived backgrounds, from more than 40% to around 30% for both English and Maths.

⇨ 16-year-olds: 7% of pupils in England obtained fewer than five GCSEs or equivalent in 2009/10. This proportion has fallen in each year since 2004/05. By contrast, the proportion between the late 1990s and the early 2000s had remained unchanged.

⇨ One in ten 16- to 18-year-olds are not in education, employment or training.

⇨ The number of permanent exclusions has fallen by a third over the last six years.

Health

⇨ Health inequalities associated with class, income or deprivation are pervasive and can be found in all aspects of health, from infant death to the risk of mental ill-health. The limited information on progress over time (infant death, low birthweight) shows no sign that they are shrinking.

⇨ Men aged 25–64 from routine or manual backgrounds are twice as likely to die as those from managerial or professional backgrounds and there are also sizeable differences for women. Scotland has by far the highest proportion of premature deaths for both men and women.

⇨ Adults in the poorest fifth of the income distribution are much more likely to be at risk of developing a mental illness as those on average incomes.

⇨ Two-fifths of adults aged 45–64 on below-average incomes have a limiting long-standing illness or disability, more than twice the rate for those on above-average incomes.

⇨ Children from manual social backgrounds are 35% more likely to die as infants than children from non-manual social backgrounds.

⇨ Babies from manual social backgrounds are somewhat more likely to be of low birthweight than those from non-manual social backgrounds.

⇨ Teenage motherhood is eight times as common amongst those from manual social backgrounds as for those from professional backgrounds.

⇨ Five-year-olds in Wales and Scotland have, on average, more than twice as many missing, decayed or filled teeth as five-year-olds in the West Midlands.

Crime

⇨ Both burglaries and violent crimes have halved over the last decade.

⇨ Households with no household insurance are more than three times as likely to be burgled as those with insurance. Half of those on low income do not have any household insurance compared with one in five households on average incomes.

Housing

⇨ 5% of people live in overcrowded conditions. Overcrowding is four times as prevalent in social rented housing as in owner-occupation.

⇨ The number of newly homeless households has fallen by three-quarters since 2003. Although most prevalent in London and the West Midlands, homelessness is to be found throughout the country.

⇨ Although now rising sharply, the number of new social housing dwellings over the last decade has been well below that required to keep up with demographic change.

⇨ Although poorer households remain more likely to lack central heating, the proportion who did so in 2003/04 (the latest data available) was actually less than that for households on average incomes in 1999/2000.

⇨ A third of homes in England were classified as non-decent in 2008.

⇨ Both overall and among those in low income, single-person households are much more likely to be in fuel poverty than other household types.

⇨ The number of mortgage repossessions fell in 2010, having risen sharply in the period from 2004 to 2009.

Disability

⇨ Around a third of all disabled adults aged 25 to retirement are living in low-income households. This is twice the rate of that for non-disabled adults.

⇨ The main reason why so many disabled people are in low-income households is their high levels of worklessness. 60% of disabled working-age adults are not in paid work compared to only 15% of their non-disabled counterparts. A third of these people – one million people – say that they want to work but that they have not been able to find a job.

⇨ At all levels of qualification, the proportion of disabled people who lack, but want, paid work is much greater than for their non-disabled counterparts.

⇨ Three-quarters of working-age people receiving a key out-of-work benefit for two years or more are sick or disabled.

⇨ Two-fifths of all adults aged 45–64 on below-average incomes have a limiting long-standing illness or disability, more than twice the rate for those on above-average incomes.

'Around a third of all disabled adults aged 25 to retirement are living in low-income households'

Ethnic minorities

⇨ Two-fifths of people from ethnic minorities live in low-income households, twice the rate for white people.

⇨ For all ethnic groups, the proportion of people who are in low-income households is slightly lower than a decade ago.

⇨ Within this, there are big variations by ethnic group. For example, more than half of people from Bangladeshi and Pakistani ethnic backgrounds live in low-income households. By contrast, 20% of people from white ethnic backgrounds live in low-income households, as do 30% of people from Indian and Black Caribbean ethnic backgrounds.

⇨ The differences are particularly great for families where at least one adult is in paid work: in these families, around 65% of Bangladeshis, 50% of Pakistanis and 30% of Black Africans are in low-income households, much higher than the 10–20% for White British, White Other, Indians and Black Caribbeans.

- A quarter of working-age Bangladeshi, Black Caribbean and Black African households are workless.

- Around a third of Bangladeshis and Pakistanis are not in paid work and say that they do not want paid work, a much higher proportion than that for any other ethnic group. Most Bangladeshi and Pakistani women are not in paid work.

- Almost half of all Bangladeshis and Pakistanis earn less than £7 per hour. Bangladeshis and Pakistanis have both the lowest work rates and, once in work, the highest likelihood of low pay.

- At both 11 and 16, deprived white British boys are more likely to fail to reach educational thresholds than either deprived white British girls or deprived boys or girls from any other ethnic group.

- Black Caribbean pupils are three times as likely to be excluded from school as white pupils.

- Black young adults are four times as likely as white young adults to be in prison.

- The above information is reprinted with kind permission from The Poverty Site. Visit www.poverty.org.uk for further information on this and other subjects.

Report shows many over-60s are 'just getting by'

An Age UK report compiled by income experts at Loughborough University has revealed many over–60s are only just able to afford the basics to get by, with some skipping meals in order to make ends meet.

The report *Living on a Low Income in Later Life,* and a subsequent ICM poll, have shown nearly one in ten (9%) older people admit to be either 'finding it difficult' or 'really struggling' to manage on their income. An estimated 4.5 million (33%) can only just afford to buy the basics.

'typically, pensioners on low incomes find life tough but are "coping" '

Experts in the University's Centre for Research in Social Policy (CRSP) carried out in-depth interviews with individuals and focus groups to gain a detailed understanding of people's experiences of living on a low income in later life.

CRSP Head of Income Studies Donald Hirsch explains:

'Our research shows that, typically, pensioners on low incomes find life tough but are "coping". Older people with limited means are often good at making their money stretch, but this can create a huge amount of stress and anxiety.

'It may mean always having to shop around for the best deal, having little to spend on small treats that can make life easier, and living in fear of debt and hardship if prices rise or a service is withdrawn.

'And real hardship for pensioners still does exist: some pensioners in Britain today are still not heating their homes properly, or skipping meals in order to make ends meet.'

People interviewed talk of cutting back, doing without and making do while at the same time worrying about the cost of energy bills and buying food.

The report highlights some examples of 'making do' such as just using a hob or microwave rather that replacing a broken oven and boiling a kettle for washing rather than heating water in a boiler. While those interviewed by researchers talk of seeking out the best bargains when food shopping and timing their shopping for the end of the day when products are marked down.

Most older people do everything they can to avoid getting into debt, and with hard work and effort they often manage day to day, but many are fearful of the future.

Michelle Mitchell, Charity Director at Age UK says:

'Living on a low income is hard work. Currently there are 1.8 million people living in poverty but our polling suggests that many above the official poverty line are finding life hard.

'Older people tend to show a great deal of resilience in managing their money and eke out their income, but the report demonstrates exactly how emotionally draining it is for older people to constantly survive on a lower income and how many are fearful of the future in the current economic climate.'

25 January 2012

- The above information is reprinted with kind permission from Loughborough University. Please visit www.loughborough.ac.uk.

The Welfare Reform Bill is the biggest benefits shake-up in 60 years

At the heart of this legislations are two key measures – the creation of a 'universal credit' and a budget cut of £18 billion.

By Randeep Ramesh

The Welfare Reform Bill, due for its second reading at the House of Lords on 13 September, is the biggest reshaping of the welfare state in six decades. At the heart of the radical Bill are two key measures. One is to collapse almost all the subsidies paid to poor people – ranging from income support to housing benefit – into a new universal credit. This aims to remove the benefit traps that see some people lose 90p in every extra pound they earn as means-tested benefits are withdrawn. The second is to pay for this by cutting £18 billion from the welfare budget over the next four years. Given the size and scope of the Bill, almost no group has been left untouched by the radical changes that the Government is pushing through. The most contentious are:

Childcare

The OECD says Britain has some of the most expensive childcare in the developed world and given the Bill's emphasis on making work pay, there has been astonishment at the Government's slashing of the cash made available to working parents under the Bill. Parents used to be reimbursed for up to 80% of £300 a week for childcare costs – so they could recoup up to £240 for two or more children, depending on their income. The Government is considering two options under the universal credit, beginning in 2013, that would further reduce childcare support. The first would mean parents could claim no more than £150.50 a week; the second would give them back just £136. This appears not to pass the 'family test' that David Cameron said last month would apply to any new policy to ensure Britain was the most family-friendly country in the world.

Free school meals

Under the old system a child would get free school meals if the parents were on certain benefits, such as jobseeker's allowance. However, the universal credit system does not distinguish between those in or out of work. Despite the Bill having been passed through Parliament there is still no level of benefits set below which children will receive free school meals.

End of the piggy-bank Welfare State

One of the most significant but little-heralded changes is that the Welfare State should no longer be regarded as a piggy bank. In the past the public were told that by paying into national insurance, they would be guaranteed benefits should they fall on hard times. Instead, the Government will limit its new 'employment and support allowance' to a year for those who have been assessed as capable of being able to be work-ready. This single change saves more than £5 billion. It will affect 700,000 people, according to the Government's own impact assessment, among them 7,000 cancer patients who could see cuts of up to £94 a week. Although Labour leader Ed Miliband and Cameron clashed over the issue, there's been no stepping back from the Government.

Underoccupation

Live in the north and have a home with a disabled person which has an unused bedroom? Then you stand to lose more than £500 a year in housing benefit. In one of the most draconian welfare cuts of recent years, 670,000 households – of which 430,000 are home to a disabled person – will be asked to make up the difference between a shrinking welfare payment and their rent for the first time in decades. About a quarter of all households affected are in the north.

1 September 2011

⇨ The above article originally appeared in *the Guardian*. Visit www.guardian.co.uk for further information.

The impact of the current Government's reforms on poverty

Information from the Institute for Fiscal Studies.

Our results suggest that the Coalition Government's reforms have no discernible impact on absolute and relative child poverty in 2011/12. Taking all children and working-age individuals together, they slightly increase relative poverty, by about 100,000.

In 2012/13, we estimate that the Coalition Government's reforms act to increase relative poverty by about 100,000 children, 100,000 working-age parents and 100,000 working-age adults without children; and they act to increase absolute poverty by about 200,000 children, 100,000 working-age parents and 100,000 working-age adults without children. This conclusion is at odds with the Coalition Government's claim that its reforms will not have a 'measurable' impact on child poverty in 2012/13, although it should be noted that a difference of 100,000 is the smallest that would be measured in the official poverty figures. The discrepancy is entirely accounted for by the fact that we have modelled the Government's planned reforms to Local Housing Allowance, whereas the Treasury did not.

In 2013/14, we estimate that Coalition reforms act to increase absolute poverty by about 300,000 children, 200,000 working-age parents and 300,000 working-age adults without children, and relative poverty by about 200,000 children, 200,000 working-age parents and 200,000 working-age adults without children. The reason that Coalition reforms do more to increase absolute than relative poverty in 2013/14 is that they reduce median income, and hence the relative poverty line, in 2013/14.

We have no way of knowing precisely how a different, hypothetical government would have chosen to rebalance the public finances had it won the 2010 general election. We have simply attempted to quantify the effect of the Coalition Government's reforms relative to the situation where it had continued with the tax and benefit plans it inherited from the previous administration. Therefore, to say that Coalition reforms are poverty-increasing in 2013/14 is not to say that poverty in 2013/14 would necessarily have been lower under a different government. We have also taken as given the expected macroeconomic environment. If the Coalition Government's reforms affect macroeconomic variables such as earnings and employment, then that could affect poverty rates.

In the longer term, the Government's planned Universal Credit has the potential to affect substantially the outlook for poverty through various channels, such as financial work incentives, take-up rates of means-tested benefits and the direct impact on benefit entitlements. Future analysis by IFS researchers will look in detail at the prospects for poverty beyond 2013/14, and how they relate to the proposed phase-in of the Universal Credit which begins in October 2013.

December 2010

⇨ The above information is from the Institute for Fiscal Studies. Please visit www.ifs. org.uk for further information or visit http://www.ifs.org.uk/publications/5373 to view the original publication.

UK: Struggling families face astronomical interest on loans

The queues forming outside credit unions to arrange loans show the extra stress that Christmas is bringing to already hard-pressed workers and their families in the UK.

Credit unions are co-operatives controlled by their members and have to have a 'common bond'. These used to be for workers from one factory, business or social club, but that remit has now widened. They have seen their customer base increase by over 20 per cent in the last year. Members do not get a loan straight away but have to save for a period with the union and then, if agreed, they can have a loan at a low interest rate.

The sole benefit of using the co-operative credit unions for many is that they will not face the astronomical interest repayments that some loan firms charge. 'Pay Day' loans are the most notorious with interest rates of 5,000 per cent if the whole amount is not repaid in one month. The firms involved excuse their rates by claiming that they represent a penalty because the loan was only meant to be short-term, hence its name.

However, when faced with repayment difficulties many borrowers are offered 'rollovers', to extend their loan for months at a time, incurring huge costs. One £80 loan escalated into £600 over a couple of months. Research by Consumer Focus last year showed the number of payday loan users rose from 300,000 in 2006 to 1.2 million in 2009. That figure has now doubled to four million, according to some recent estimates, as the Conservative-Liberal Democrat Government's austerity measures bite, with rising unemployment, inflation and pay cuts and freezes.

Any search engine throws up dozens of different payday companies offering decisions in 15 minutes. People are assured that the money will appear in their bank accounts straight away, and that no credit checks will be made.

The companies go under the salubrious names of QuickQuid, Check'n Go, Wonga, etc. The Consumer's Association estimates that the payday loan industry is worth £1.5 billion. Lenders advertise the ease of repayments that will be deducted from customers' bank accounts on payment day, potentially leaving them unable to meet other, more important, costs such as their mortgage. Over 18,000 homes were repossessed in the first six months of the year, while the number of mortgages in arrears stands at 78,000 – all potential repossessions that could surface next year.

Radio 4's *Money Box* programme has revealed that the major high street banks are also charging huge costs for unauthorised overdrafts for customers who go over their limit. A customer going into an overdraft of £100 for 28 days without the consent of Santander would repay £200, for example. That is the equivalent annualised percentage rate, or APR, of 819,100 per cent.

A representative of the British Banking Association said that using APRs to calculate the cost of unauthorised borrowing was a 'mathematical manipulation' because the fees are representative of borrowing on an overdraft facility, not for borrowing the specific amount of money from the bank. Mike Dailly, from the Govan Law Centre, said the Government must review unauthorised overdraft charges. 'What we've got here is banks with equivalent APRs of nearly one million per cent,' he said. 'It really is eye-watering.'

Other loan companies try to distance their businesses from the payday companies, but on close examination their interest repayments can be as much as 2,500 per cent for late payers. Their web sites encourage the use of the loans for non–essentials such as new cars and house renovations to finance a lifestyle out of their grasp.

Most loan companies require a bank account and pay cheque, so the only route left for the unemployed is the door-to-door money lenders of many years standing. They used to offer 'cheques' for use in school wear shops or for specific clothes retailers, but now it is mostly cash loans. Catering for the unemployed and those with a bad credit history, they make arrangements to call personally to collect the money when the benefit has been paid.

The Citizens Advice Service is usually the first port of call for people seeking help when they get into arrears. Those using the service in Dumfries and Galloway, Scotland, for example, have recorded levels of debt far in excess of previous years. Its annual report has revealed that in the last 12 months the organisation helped nearly 1,300 clients who collectively owed almost £28 million. This has led to the largest debt recovery firm in Scotland, Mackenzie Hall, doubling its workforce at the Kilmarnock call centre to cope with the surge in bad debts.

Another phenomenon bred by the recession is the logbook loan for those who own – or almost own – a car outright that is worth more than £200 and is less than ten years old. A person places the logbook with the company, signs a bill of sale – which is claimed will only be used as a last resort – and receives a loan.

In some instances people can expect a repayment of £2,000 on an £800 loan.

The concept of logbook loans stems from legislation dating back to Victorian times – the Bills of Sale Act in 1878 and its amendment in 1882. It states that the item on which the loan is secured can be seized and sold if the borrower defaults, and the borrower can still be pursued if there is any shortfall when the item is sold.

The companies involved frequently repossess vehicles on the first late payment and are less than scrupulous in their bookkeeping. They also charge for every reminder issued, at the rate of £12 a phone call or letter. These charges are aggressively pursued and expected to be paid in full at the end of the agreement, and some borrowers find themselves facing bills of £800 purely for administration charges. The firms take the borrower to court for these amounts, putting further pressure and in some cases risking their homes, as more loans are secured on their property when court fees are added.

Almost 40,000 loans of this type were made in the year March 2009 for sums amounting to £30 million. Because of the tactics of these companies, the Department for Business Innovation and Skills (BIS) is carrying out a 12-week consultation on what it calls the 'archaic' and expensive method of borrowing, after which the practice is expected to be banned.

Banning these parasitic firms alone, however, is not the answer to the financial situation in which workers and their families find themselves. The Government is stripping away the safety nets associated with the welfare state, aggressively attacking unemployment and working families' benefits, forcing more and more people to turn to loans to supplement their resources.

23 December 2011

⇨ Information from the World Socialist Web Site. Please visit http://wsws.org for further information.

Charity condemns 'unequal' England

A Church of England charity has described England as one of the most unequal countries in the western world as research was published showing an 'alarming disparity' between the richest and poorest neighbourhoods in the country.

Nine out of ten of the poorest communities – five of them in Liverpool – are in the north west of England with the tenth in Middlesbrough in the north east, found research by the Church Urban Fund (CUF).

Only two of top ten least-deprived communities were in the north of England – in Wheldrake, York and Alderley Edge, Cheshire, with Camberley Heatherside, Surrey, heading the list of the least-deprived communities in England.

The findings were calculated at Church of England parish level with an online method devised by the fund using data on life expectancy and poverty rates among children, pensioners and people of working age.

The research showed life expectancy for men in South Shore, Blackpool, was as low as 66 years, with 62% of children and 52% of pensioners living in poverty in Toxteth (east) Liverpool, which ranked as the most deprived community in the country.

In Camberley Heatherside in Surrey, only 6% of children and 3% of pensioners are living in poverty, the research showed. The fund said that the research had shown how close some of the most affluent areas are to communities suffering from extreme deprivation.

An area of Harpenden, Hertfordshire, ranks as the seventh most affluent in the country but is based just six miles from the community of Farley Hill in Luton, one of the most deprived neighbourhoods in England, said the CUF, which works to tackle poverty in England by providing debt counselling and homeless shelters. Paul Hackwood, chairman of the CUF trustees, said: 'We live in one of the most unequal countries in the western world, where babies born within a few miles of one another can have widely differing life expectancies - of ten years or more.

'We urge people to go online and try out the tool and find out where their local community ranks in terms of poverty indicators.

'We hope it will create a much greater awareness of poverty in England and bring people from affluent and less affluent areas together to think about what could be done to support those that are living in poverty.'

21 May 2012

⇨ The above information is reprinted with kind permission from The Press Association. Visit www.pressassociation.com for more information.

Robin Hood Tax

You'll have heard of Robin Hood. Took from the rich, gave to the poor. Looked a bit like Russell Crowe. Well, Robin Hood Taxes follow the same logic. Except for 'rich' read 'financial sector' and for 'poor' read 'public services, the fight against climate change and poor people in the UK and overseas'.

In the UK over 13 million people live in poverty. That's one in five who have to choose between switching on the heating or buying enough food to put a meal on the table.

Crisis in the UK

Britain is the fifth richest country in the world – so how did this happen? Inequality and an inflexible benefit system make it difficult for families in the UK to break the poverty cycle. Designed in the 1960s the benefit system is unable to cope with the part-time work and temporary contracts so commonplace today.

Inequality is rife and many don't get the opportunity to flourish. Take a look at exam results: children living in poverty here still do far worse at school than wealthier children.

Since 2002 the poorest tenth have become £9 a week poorer (a lot if you can barely get by). While the richest tenth have £94 more a week.

And that includes people who have jobs. There are hundreds of thousands of people in paid work who are struggling to get by. People who make a huge contribution to society like care workers, class–room assistants that end up juggling two or three jobs just to make ends meet.

The fact that it's so hard to escape the poverty trap doesn't mean the problem is big – it means it's endemic.

A Robin Hood Tax could help us create the society we all wish to live in. We may be in the shadow of recession, but we shouldn't wait until recovery dawns to fight poverty.

The Robin Hood Tax could raise billions every year to help fight poverty in the UK. It could help end child poverty, reform the welfare system, end fuel poverty and protect frontline services.

The reality

Being poor in the UK means the same as it does around the world. Struggling to get by. Fretting over your next meal. Overcrowded accommodation. Constant illness. Low life expectancy. Worry.

It means choking back tears when you have to send your kids to school without breakfast. It means dreading the moment they come back needing money for a new book. It means choosing between cooking a healthy meal or paying the gas bill.

And – just like anywhere else – it also means constant stigma. A sense that you're powerless to change your situation. A battle to access – and influence – the local services that could really help you turn your life around.

Right now, across the UK, 13 million people are faced with that reality.

Thirteen million. That's one in five. In the fifth richest country on earth. And the gap between rich and poor is growing.

What Robin can do

There are a lot of reasons for this crazy situation. It won't change overnight. But a major part of the blame for the ongoing inequality lies with the politicians we've elected. And, unsurprisingly, they're also at the heart of the solution – with a little help from Robin Hood.

After all, it's a government's responsibility to support its citizens. That means protecting people from poverty. It means preventing the kind of inequality that has resulted in life expectancy

in Glasgow dropping to 54 – the same as in Malawi.

It also means helping people when they are struggling, so they have a better chance of building a better future. And it means providing a basic system of universal welfare, alongside targeted support for those in real trouble.

But it's estimated that budget cuts will actually result in 38,000 extra deaths over the next decade. Read that, and suddenly the cuts to essential services and the desperate desire to reduce the budget deficit seem much more dangerous.

Put simply, this Government is at risk of abandoning its duty to provide social protection. But the Robin Hood Tax could change everything.

It could raise billions every year to help fight poverty in the UK. It could help end child poverty, reform the welfare system, end fuel poverty and protect vital frontline services.

Global economic crisis

The effects of the global economic crisis have been felt around the world and we're all tightening our belts. And the poor countries, who did nothing to cause the crisis, are feeling the effects.

Imagine for a minute that you've already spend 80% of your income on food – even the slightest price increase or drop in your income could mean you go without food for a few days. What would you do?

Credit crunch, financial crash, recession, global downturn – whatever you choose to call it – the economic crisis that began in 2008 set in motion a troubling chain of events.

As global markets collapsed, there was far less money to go round. People all over the world bought less stuff. Developing countries' exports fell and millions of jobs disappeared.

This crisis has created a financial 'hole' for the 56 poorest countries, mostly in Africa. Zambia has slashed its health spending, while Niger and Mali have taken the axe to their schools budget. Middle income countries like China, India and Brazil remain relatively unharmed. The World Bank estimates that two million children will die as a direct impact of the crisis.

'a fire fuelled in wealthy countries also burnt millions of poor people'

Poor people are struggling – but they're toughing it out, fighting to drag themselves out of poverty. But the credit crunch is not over yet and the impact of this downturn will hit them harder and longer.

The reality

The effects of the banking crisis on developing countries didn't get a huge amount of coverage in the UK. Understandably enough, the focus here was on the impact here, as the actions of a small minority of bankers wreaked havoc on the UK economy.

But, unsurprisingly, a fire fuelled in wealthy countries also burnt millions of poor people – and continues to do so.

There are the inevitable pitfalls of globalisation, for starters. Spending falls in the UK. People buy fewer clothes. Shops order fewer clothes. Orders fall in factories in poor countries. People are laid off and can't find alternative work. And suddenly the global economic crisis hits the market stall holder who used to sell lunches to the people in factories. And so on and so on.

But the crisis has also had a profound effect on poor countries at the macro level. The UN has estimated that between 47 and 84 million more people have either remained extremely poor or been forced into poverty by the economic downturn. And an Oxfam study of 56 of the world's poorest countries found that it wasn't just wealthy states that responded to the crisis by borrowing – poor countries did the same thing.

They were forced to borrow locally at high interest rates, or to run down financial reserves. As a result, deep spending cuts have now inevitably followed – and education, social protection and pensions have all been hit.

Or, to put it another way, some of the world's poorest people have had their chances of a better future – and the safety net provided by state welfare – swept from under them by a cluster of financial organisations whose only concern was their bottom line.

What Robin can do

In the face of this crisis, rumblings are increasing about cutting foreign aid. The UK Government deserves a lot of credit for ring-fencing its aid budget, but in many places aid is being reduced or concentrated in fewer countries. Another worrying trend is for countries to focus on only one or two of the Millennium Development Goals – an unacceptable response because the MDGs are so deeply interlinked.

So what's the solution? Well, it makes sense for poor countries to generate more revenue by raising taxes on income and property, as well as on foreign investment. In that way, the poorest people in the poorest countries can be protected from tax increases.

But the real solution lies with Robin Hood Taxes. People in developing countries did nothing to cause the crisis but are facing its consequences. Think of it as ending up with a thumping hangover without even being invited to the party.

So it's time for those most responsible to pay up. Robin Hood Taxes are truly progressive – generating revenue only from those who can afford to pay and who have a moral obligation to do so.

A Robin Hood Tax could raise billions every year to help those hit hardest by the economic crisis, at home and abroad.

Everything you need to know about Robin

In a nutshell, the big idea behind the Robin Hood Tax is to generate billions of pounds – hopefully even hundreds of billions of pounds. That money will fight poverty in the UK and overseas. It will tackle climate change. And it will come from fairer taxation of the financial sector.

A tiny tax on the financial sector can generate £20 billion annually in the UK alone. That's enough to protect schools and hospitals. Enough to stop massive cuts across the public sector. Enough to build new lives around the world – and to deal with the new climate challenges our world is facing.

'It's time for justice. It's time for justice for ordinary families and businesses'

As a result of the financial crisis, the International Monetary Fund (IMF) has calculated UK Government debt will be 40% higher. That 40% equates to £737 billion, or £28,000 for every taxpayer in the country. Having to pay back that debt means cuts in vital services on which millions of people around the country rely.

Total cost to the UK of the financial crisis in terms of lost output according to the IMF was 27% of 2008 GDP.

So it's time for justice. It's time for justice for ordinary families and businesses. For the one in five British families faced with a choice between buying food or paying the heating bill. For the millions of people around the world forced into poverty by a financial crisis they did absolutely nothing to bring about.

The Robin Hood Tax is justice. The banks can afford it. The systems are in place to collect it. It won't affect ordinary members of the public, their bank accounts or their savings. It's fair, it's timely, and it's possible.

It is an idea for which the time has come.

Who's behind it?

The Robin Hood Tax campaign started as an idea. People loved it. We became a movement. And we're still growing.

We're committed to reducing poverty and tackling climate change by taxing financial transactions.

We believe it's time to rewrite the contract between banks and society.

We are charities, green groups, trade unions, celebrities, religious leaders and politicians.

We are world leaders – President Sarkozy of France, Chancellor Merkel of Germany, among others.

We are businesspeople – FSA Chairman Lord Turner, financier George Soros, entrepreneur extraordinaire Warren Buffet.

We are economists – Nobel Prize winners Joseph Stiglitz and Paul Krugman, Earth Institute Director Jeffrey Sachs and 1,000 other economists from across the world.

We are 262,000 Facebook friends, and tens of thousands of people taking action around the UK. We are over 115 organisations, including charities like Oxfam, Barnardo's and Friends of the Earth, all the major trade unions and faith organisations such as the Salvation Army.

We are part of a movement of campaigns in more than 25 countries around the world with millions of supporters.

We are a force to be reckoned with, and we're demanding justice.

⇨ Information from The Robin Hood Tax. Please visit www. robinhoodtax.org.uk for further information.

© 2010 The Robin Hood Tax

What is fuel poverty?

Questions about high energy bills, fuel poverty and children living in cold homes.

What is a cold home?

The World Health Organization recommends indoor temperatures are maintained at 21 degrees in living rooms and 18 degrees in bedrooms for at least 9 hours a day.

What is fuel poverty?

Fuel poverty is defined as having to spend 10% or more of a household's income to heat their home to an adequate standard of warmth.

Being in fuel poverty is made up of three factors:

1. the energy efficiency of the house (which determines, in part, how expensive it will be to heat)

2. the cost of heating fuel

3. the household income (which determines how much 10% would be).

This means:

⇨ not all households that are income poor are fuel poor (as they might live in a good, energy efficient home)

⇨ factors other than income poverty can be tackled to reduce fuel poverty (such as fuel efficiency measures like insulation and double glazing)

⇨ not all fuel poor houses are income poor (households living in very old/poor/draughty housing stock may have to spend a larger proportion of income on heating).

How many households are fuel poor?

Latest figures estimate that six million households in the UK are now living in fuel poverty. This means that over one million families with children are struggling to keep their homes warm.

Figures have risen sharply over the past few years, largely due to the increase in fossil fuel prices around the world.

How are high energy costs hitting the poorest families (those living on less than £12,000 a year)?

Save the Children carried out research published in December 2011 which demonstrates how families are being hit by the cost of energy bills:

⇨ Almost half (45%) of parents have said they are considering cutting back on food in order to pay their energy bills this winter.

⇨ 54% of all parents are worried that their children's health will suffer because their house is too cold this winter.

⇨ 71% of parents are worried that their winter energy bill will push them into debt.

How much do people pay for their energy?

The average dual fuel bill (for both gas and electricity from the same provider) is now £1,345 per year.

Many consumers – in particular poorer consumers without bank accounts to pay by direct debit or with pre-payment meters due to arrears – are not eligible for the cheapest deals and so pay higher rates for their fuel.

How is children's health affected by cold homes?

Children's health and well-being can be badly affected by living in inadequately heated housing:

They are more than twice as likely to suffer from a variety of respiratory problems, such as asthma and bronchitis, as children living in warm homes.

More than one in four adolescents living in cold housing are at risk of multiple mental health problems – the figure is one in 20 of those who have always lived in warm housing.

Cold housing also negatively affects how children perform at school and their emotional well-being.

Many of the most vulnerable members of society, including disabled children, spend longer in the home than most, and require the heating on all day. According to a survey from Contact a Family, two thirds of families with disabled children struggle to pay their energy bills in the winter time.

How can people living in fuel poverty be helped?

The easiest one of the three factors making up fuel poverty to change is energy efficiency.

Making homes more energy efficient is a long-term, sustainable solution, which will allow people to use less energy to heat their homes adequately. This will have a positive impact on carbon emissions and on fuel bills.

What is a fuel efficient home?

Some people call fixing houses so that energy is not wasted, 'fuel poverty proofing'. This means that the house is so energy efficient that people do not need to spend a lot of their income to keep warm.

If all properties in England were in band B, it would raise 83% of households out of fuel poverty. Half of the existing housing stock in our country falls well below this standard and most homes built before the 1920s fall within bands F and G. Current building regulations require a SAP rating between 65–81 (top of band D and above) for newly built houses.

How can energy efficient homes help the Government?

Energy efficient homes will reduce carbon emissions from our houses, helping the environment and helping the UK meet its target of cutting CO_2 emissions by 34% of 1990 levels by 2020. They will also help the Government to meet its legal duty to eliminate fuel poverty by 2016.

How much does it cost to make a home fuel efficient?

The vast majority (84%) of the UK's least energy efficient homes could be brought up to near-average standards for less than £3,000. (This would bring them up to band E. The average for homes in UK is now band D.)

A small proportion of properties will be hard to make decent and will cost over £5,000 to improve.

Some of these measures can be taken by individuals and some need professional contractors to undertake.

Why should we make our homes energy efficient?

As well as cutting energy bills, making homes energy efficient ensures we are not wasting energy and contributing to climate change.

Domestic energy use is responsible for around a quarter of the UK's CO_2 emissions (over 70% through space and water heating). Poor insulation means around £1 in every £4 currently spent heating homes is wasted.

How do people pay for these improvements?

Currently people can pay for these energy efficiency measures themselves if they can afford it. There are also taxpayer–funded schemes to install energy efficiency measures in homes occupied by low-income or vulnerable households, such as Warm Front. In addition, energy companies have schemes to support improvements in some households.

From autumn 2012, there will be a new scheme available called the Green Deal. This is not a taxpayer–funded scheme but allows private energy companies to provide financing for customers (both domestic and commercial) to make energy efficiency improvements and reduce heating bills. The Energy Company Obligation (ECO) will support those householders (on lower incomes or with properties that are more difficult and expensive to improve) that do not qualify for the Green Deal.

Notes

Energy Performance Certificates (EPCs) show how energy efficient a property is, using rating bands from A–G. Band A is most efficient and band G is least efficient.

⇨ Information from *National Children's Bureau (2011) Some questions answered about high energy bills, fuel poverty and children living in cold homes.* London: National Children's Bureau

© *National Children's Bureau*

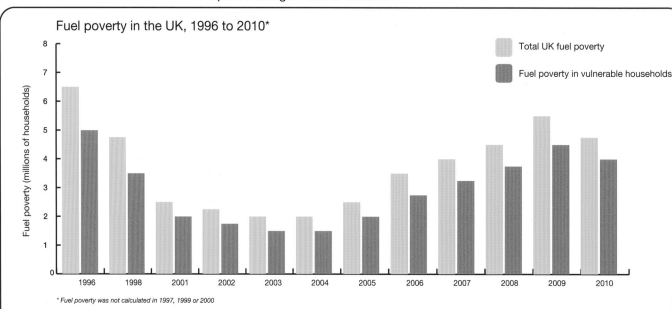

Fuel poverty in the UK, 1996 to 2010*

Legend: Total UK fuel poverty; Fuel poverty in vulnerable households

Y-axis: Fuel poverty (millions of households)

X-axis: 1996, 1998, 2001, 2002, 2003, 2004, 2005, 2006, 2007, 2008, 2009, 2010

* Fuel poverty was not calculated in 1997, 1999 or 2000

Source: Annual report on fuel poverty statistics, 2012. *Department of Energy and Climate Change. May 2012. © Crown Copyright*

Food poverty on the rise as recession hits home

In 21st–century Britain, you would not expect people across the country to need food handouts to survive – particularly those with jobs. But that's exactly what Political Editor Gary Gibbon finds.

We just can't bend any lower...

Flexible workforce.

You might normally associate Salisbury with cathedrals and green wellies. But Channel 4 News visited for another reason: to find out about foodbanks.

The Trussell Trust in Salisbury is one of dozens of US-style charity operations that have grown up unannounced around the country, handing out parcels of food to people unable to put a meal on the table.

Tens of thousands each year get food parcels – mostly referred by GPs, health visitors, police, schools.

Poverty

But there is a new phenomenon being reported by the foodbanks which throws light on life in Britain for many today. They say their biggest growing cohort of people coming for help getting food on the table are people who either have an income, or people in a household where there is an income.

In-work poverty was a growing phenomenon in the UK – the latest estimate is that 53 per cent of working-age households in poverty have at least one working adult. This is around 2.3 million households, after factoring in housing costs. What the foodbank experience suggests is that these individuals are finding they plummet into crisis situations suddenly and more frequently.

One woman who has been forced to use the foodbanks in Salisbury told Channel 4 News: 'Because I've always worked, I never expected to be in that position where I would be so grateful for somebody else giving us some food.'

Sometimes, the emergency happens because agency work suddenly dries up – a construction worker Channel 4 News spoke to can be on £800 one month and £170 the next.

He said: 'In the climate we're in at the moment, sometimes I'm doing it on a regular basis and it's difficult and I find it embarrassing. You just feel so small.'

The fixed outgoings are geared more to the better income and are stretched to destruction by the plummeting one. To some, the labour market flexibilities introduced – starting in the 1980s – seem to be showing a lot of flexibility in one direction. Estimates on the number of agency workers across the country vary from around 260,000 (the Government's Labour Force Survey) to 1.25 million (the agency trade body the Recruitment and Employment Confederation).

Crisis situation

Other factors that seem to trigger crisis situations for the working poor are self-employed individuals whose income is erratic, and workers forced onto lower working hours by their employers.

The latest National Institute of Economic and Social Research revealed that 97 per cent of the jobs created since the recession ended are part-time.

But the Department for Work and Pensions' figures breakdown seems to show that 1.2 million of them actually wanted to work more hours but were being kept at lower working hours to keep the company ticking over or to keep company costs down. As unemployment figures underline, it's not the right time to go hunting in the job market, so people stay put and hope for better times.

For some needing food parcels the problem is accumulated debts and credit card payments eating into their disposable income. The personal debt figures for the UK tell you how widespread that must be. What all said was that the costs of petrol, food and rent – the basics – are having a lethal effect.

Political Editor Gary Gibbon said: 'Tax credits don't seem to protect these people. The market doesn't want to pay them at the rate for the hours they want to work. Politicians have told workers that getting into work is the promised land, but what if it isn't? And what if the economic recovery doesn't float all boats?'

⇨ A version of this article was first published by channel4.com/news. Visit www.channel4.com/news for further information.

© Channel 4 2012

Why end child poverty?

Information from Child Poverty Action Group.

Why end child poverty?

The extent of poverty in the UK has changed dramatically.

The number of people living in poverty more than doubled between 1979 and 1999.

Since then the Government has managed to reduce the overall numbers of people living in poverty; however, almost 13 million people still live below the poverty line.

The face of poverty has also changed. Children have replaced pensioners as the most 'at-risk' group. There are now four million children living in poverty (27%) with even higher rates in urban areas such as London, Birmingham and Manchester.

Poverty experienced during childhood can have a profound and lasting impact on the child and their family. It often sets in motion a deepening spiral of social exclusion, creating problems with education, employment, mental and physical health and social interaction.

The Government has pledged to meet targets for reducing child poverty to match the best performing countries in Europe by 2020, but those goals are now in jeopardy due to the decision of the Coalition Government to make children and families the main target of their austerity agenda.

Instead of being reduced, the independent experts at the Institute for Fiscal Studies have produced analysis that suggests the Government's taxation and welfare politics will result in an increase of the number of children in poverty by 400,000 by 2015.

Poor children are excluded from participating in society. They can't afford school trips and activities, school uniforms or warm winter clothes, are unable to go swimming, have friends round for tea or celebrate their birthdays. Many will never have a holiday.

Child poverty costs us all, both financially and socially. Children who grow up poor are more likely to leave school without qualifications, have lower employment chances, thus restricting their ability to get a good job and financially contribute to society.

It has been estimated hat child poverty currently costs society £25 billion each year (Joseph Rowntree Foundation). Child poverty is therefore not only a social problem, it is also a major economic cost to the UK.

We need to ensure that governments invest the resources needed to meet the 2020 targets for reducing child poverty. This requires action not just on income poverty, but also on other areas including tackling poor education outcomes, increasing the supply of living wage jobs, reducing health inequalities and providing a major increase in the supply of affordable housing.

With your support, the Campaign to End Child Poverty can pressurise ministers into taking the action necessary to ensure an end to child poverty. They have to commit the resources required to tackle the causes, as well as the symptoms, of poverty.

Key facts

⇨ Nearly four million children are living in poverty in the UK.

⇨ The proportion of children living in poverty grew from one in ten in 1979 to one in three in 1998. Today, 27 per cent of children in Britain are living in poverty.

⇨ The UK has one of the worst rates of child poverty in the industrialised world.

⇨ The majority (58 per cent) of poor children live in a household where at least one adult works.

⇨ 40 per cent of poor children live in a household headed by a lone parent. The majority of poor children (57 per cent) live in a household headed by a couple.

⇨ 38 per cent of children in poverty are from families with three or more children.

⇨ Since 1999, when the previous Government pledged to end child poverty, a million children have been lifted out of poverty.

Source: Figures for 'after housing costs' relative low income poverty, HBAI 2010/11 DWP.

The effects

Poverty and life chances

Poverty shortens lives. A boy in Manchester can expect to live seven years less than a boy in Barnet. A girl in Manchester can expect to live six years less than a girl in Kensington Chelsea and Westminster.

Poor children are born too small; birth weight is on average 130 grams lower in children from social classes IV and V. Low birth weight is closely associated with infant death and chronic diseases in later life.

Poverty shapes children's development. Before reaching his or her second birthday, a child from a poorer family is already more likely to show a lower level of developmental attainment than a child from a better-off family.

Children aged up to 14 from unskilled families are five times more likely to die in an accident than children from professional families, and 15 times more likely to die in a fire at home.

Children growing up in poverty are more likely to leave school at 16 with fewer qualifications.

Child Poverty Act

The Child Poverty Act received Royal Assent on 25th March 2010.

The Campaign to End Child Poverty welcomes this legislation which will make tackling child poverty a priority for all governments. Giving legal force to the commitment to eradicate child poverty by 2020 is a major step forward and will compel successive governments to account for what they are doing to achieve that goal.

Now that the Child Poverty Act has become law, a Social Mobility and Child Poverty Commission is being appointed. The Commission will scrutinise the Government's progress on child poverty, publishing yearly reports and critiquing the Government's child poverty strategy.

Notes

End Child Poverty use 'after housing cost' (AHC) figures when referring to the number of children in poverty. Please be aware that other organisations may use 'before housing costs' (BHC) figures.

AHC figures are significantly higher because housing is so expensive in the UK that is can dramatically reduce the disposable income families have left to pay for other essential things. The government uses BHC for its targets, but whenever referring to the number of children 'in poverty', or 'living in poverty' (rather than specific references to the targets) End Child Poverty believe it is best practice to use the AHC figures, as this properly represents the situation faced by families.

⇨ The above information is reprinted with kind permission from Child Poverty Action Group. Please visit www.cpag.org.uk for further information.

Child Poverty Strategy

Information from the Department for Education.

A New Approach to Child Poverty: Tackling the Causes of Disadvantage and Transforming Families' Lives sets out the Government's approach to tackling poverty for this Parliament and up to 2020. At its heart are strengthening families, encouraging responsibility, promoting work, guaranteeing fairness and providing support to the most vulnerable. This strategy meets the requirements set out in the Child Poverty Act 2010, focuses on improving the life chances of the most disadvantaged children, and sits alongside the Government's broader strategy to improve social mobility. The core ways to achieve this are:

⇨ A stronger focus on ensuring that families who are in work are supported to work themselves out of poverty, families who are unable to work are able to live with dignity and not entrenched in persistent poverty, and that those who can work but are not in work are provided with services that will address their particular needs and help them overcome barriers to work.

⇨ A stronger focus on improving children's future life chances, by intervening early to improve the development and attainment of disadvantaged children and young people throughout their transition to adulthood.

⇨ A stronger focus on place and delivering services as close to the family as possible, by empowering local partners and ensuring that local diversity can be recognised, and developing strong local accountability frameworks.

This strategy provides a powerful springboard for progress both towards the income targets over the long term, and towards minimising socio-economic disadvantage for children. Our more detailed measurement and monitoring – including lead indicators and gap measures – will tell us whether we are making an impact and where we need to adjust the approach.

26 April 2012

⇨ Information from the Department for Education. Please visit www. education.gov.uk for further information.

Barnardo's Child Poverty Quiz

Over the last few years the credit crunch has affected all of us. Prices are rising, businesses are closing and everyone has to watch their money more carefully. But while we all worry about our finances it is all too easy to forget about child poverty. It is often forgotten in the newspapers or on the television, so how big an issue can it be?

*Discover what you really know about child poverty by taking Barnardo's quiz below, or visit **www.barnardos.co.uk** for more information on child poverty in the UK.*

1 How many children in the UK live in poverty?

☐ 1 million
☐ 2.5 million
☐ 3.6 million

2 How much money do you think a family of four living in poverty have to survive on each week?

☐ £349
☐ £387
☐ £423

3 What is the annual cost of child poverty to the country?

☐ £25 million
☐ £2.5 billion
☐ £25 billion

4 How many poor children have at least one parent in work?

☐ 10%
☐ 20%
☐ 58%

5 What percentage of poor parents cannot keep their house warm this winter?

☐ 24%
☐ 10%
☐ 20%

6 At what age is a less able child from a rich family less likely to have overtaken a more able child from a poor family?

☐ 6
☐ 10
☐ 20

B ONUS QUESTION – the Government is on track to meet its targets for reducing child poverty.

☐ True
☐ False

Answers on page 22 ⇨

2 skint 4 school

Information from Child Poverty Action Group.

What does child poverty have to do with educational achievement?

The Government has implemented wide-ranging educational reforms and per-pupil spending levels are now up to 'record levels'. And yet the attainment gap between rich and poor pupils gets wider as they progress through the education system.

By three years old, poor children may be up to a year behind the wealthiest children in terms of cognitive development and 'school readiness'.

Wealthier pupils perform better at all stages of schooling than pupils eligible for free school meals, regardless of race or gender.

By the time they move to secondary school poorer children are on average two years behind better-off children.

High performing pupils at primary school are four times more likely to fall into low achievement by GCSEs if they are poor.

Being poor means a pupil is nearly three times as likely to fail to get at least five A–C grades at GCSE – and the grade gap with the wealthiest pupils is widening.

Just over 6% of poor pupils receiving free school meals remain at school to take A–levels, compared to around 40% of students overall.

60,000 state school pupils in the top 20% of academic performers do not go on to higher education each year.

What problems do children from poor families face?

Children do not leave the problems of social and economic inequality behind at the school gates – they carry them into the classroom:

⇨ Poor children are more likely to have health problems from birth, and to develop disabilities and special educational needs.

⇨ Families with low incomes and bad housing struggle to provide a strong learning environment at home.

⇨ A child who is stressed, hungry and stigmatised is unlikely to thrive in the classroom.

A 2003 Government study found:

⇨ Parents of secondary pupils spend on average around £1,000 on extra school costs like uniforms, trips and equipment.

⇨ 55% of low–income families find it difficult to meet extra school costs.

⇨ Pupils whose parents can't afford the cost of an activity or trip are twice as likely to pretend they do not want to do it as to tell the school they cannot afford it.

A 2007 survey of more than 1,000 parents by the School Costs Coalition found:

⇨ Over 10% said extra school costs affected their choice of school.

Why aren't things getting better?

Policy makers and political parties are focusing on the wrong areas: on endless reforms of school management structures, disciplinary ethos and ownership of schools. Core problems not being addressed include:

Schools are failing to target additional resources on the children who need it most.

⇨ Parental choice is favouring wealthier parents and generating educational inequalities.

⇨ Local authorities have more demands heaped on them, yet do not have the resources or the power to redistribute wealth to poorer families.

⇨ Less attention is focused on tackling the causes of poverty – by raising family income – than on dealing with its consequences in the classroom.

⇨ The Government is not recognising the extent to which child poverty drives educational failure and that improvements require more support for poor families.

What needs to change?

Lack of family income is damaging children's educational outcomes and making teachers' jobs much harder. Families need more money to ensure their children are well fed, warm, live in safe and secure environments and can participate in the full range of cultural and social activities outside of school. The Government must ensure all children access all parts of the education system. Reducing poverty and improving child well–being must be placed at the heart of the Government's educational agenda. Reducing child poverty and its impact through action in the following areas will reduce the educational attainment gap:

Family incomes for education

Children do not leave social and economic inequalities at the school gates – they bring them into the classroom. Being poor harms their well–being and limits their ability to learn. Poorer children are more likely to be tired, hungry and disengaged from the educational process. They often can't afford to participate in social, sporting or creative activities in the wider community. The most effective way of targeting additional funds on disadvantaged children is to make sure families receive the money they need to keep their children out of poverty and to support their education.

Homes fit for learning

A cold, cramped home without a quiet warm place to study, without equipment like books or computers, damages children's lives and educational experiences. Constant moves and temporary accommodation generate insecurity and stress. Homes fit for learning – and living – must be placed at the heart of the educational agenda.

Genuinely free education

Schools' charging policies mean that a 'free' education can cost hundreds of pounds per child. Poor families may have to pay for school trips, music lessons or revision guides. Poor children in working families may not be entitled to free school meals. Poor children in non-working families may be excluded from childcare and extended school provision because their parents do not qualify for the childcare element of working tax credit. This damages child well–being, compromises teachers and compounds educational inequalities. The Government must ensure that all children access all aspects of the educational system; and schools must ensure children are not stigmatised or excluded from any school-based activities.

Support for teachers

The most committed teacher cannot compensate the poorest children for the ill health, poor housing and lack of opportunities that blight their lives. The Government must address the causes of poverty and teachers need more support to help them cope with its consequences. Schools – and teacher training courses – must ensure

that teachers have the skills, training and specialist support they need to cope with the diverse challenges associated with child poverty.

Good schools for all

Selection – and parental 'choice' – exclude poor children from 'good' schools. This may damage children's educational experiences and aspirations in 'disadvantaged' schools. In the classroom, poor children's needs may be sacrificed to the demands of league tables or parental choice. The Government must recognise that some of its policies are generating educational inequality, and others are proving ineffective. It must do more to ensure that all schools get the best out of all the children in their care. Reducing educational charges and providing universal free school meals will help make all schools more accessible learning environments.

⇨ The above information is reprinted with kind permission from Child Poverty Action Group. Please visit www.cpag.org.uk for further information.

Barnardo's Child poverty quiz: Answers

1. An appalling 3.6 million children across the UK live in poverty. That's almost one in three children. This is unacceptable in one of the world's richest countries.

2. With just £349 a week this family are on the poverty line. This has to cover all their food, gas, electricity, water, clothes, transport, and rent. Inevitably their children will have to go without some of these basic things, and miss out on 'luxuries' such as birthday and Christmas presents. Often, they're forced into taking out expensive and inappropriate credit. In reality, four million children scrape by on even less.

3. We spend £25 billion a year trying to mitigate the impact of child poverty through services and interventions. The sooner child poverty ends, the sooner

all of society can benefit. This is the equivalent of £800 per taxpayer.

4. 58% of poor children have at least one parent in part of full-time work.

5. 24% of the poorest parents and their children in low–income households have to fight off the freezing temperatures without central heating. Shockingly, no grants are available to help the majority of these families out.

6. A child who is less able, but from a wealthy background, is likely to have overtaken a child from a poorer background at the age of six.

⇨ BONUS QUESTION – Despite the Government's pledge to halve child poverty by 2010, and to eradicate by 2020, they are not on course to achieve this. Drastic new measures

need to be introduced to get the Government to keep its promise. Barnardos is a key member of the campaign to End Child Poverty.

The good news is that you can help put a stop to child poverty. Sign up to Barnardo's e-newsletters to be kept informed of how you can be involved in our campaigns. Your support is vital to transforming the lives of all children across the UK. For more information, please email poverty@barnardos.org.uk.

⇨ Information is reprinted with kind permission from Barnardo's. Please visit their website www.barnardos.org.uk for further information on this and other subjects.

Poverty

Information from The World Bank.

At a glance

⇨ The developing world has likely attained the first Millennium Development Goal (MDG) target of halving the 1990 poverty rate by 2015. The 1990 poverty rate at the $1.25 a day poverty line in 2005 prices was nearly halved in 2008, and preliminary estimates for 2010 indicate that this MDG target was already achieved before the 2015 deadline. The international line of $1.25 a day is the average of the national poverty lines in the poorest 10–20 countries.

⇨ The share of the developing world living on less than $1.25 a day was 22 per cent in 2008, down from 43 per cent in 1990 and 52 per cent in 1981. In terms of the number of poor, 1.29 billion people lived on less than $1.25 a day in 2008, as compared to 1.91 billion in 1990 and 1.94 billion in 1981. However, even at the current rate of progress, about one billion people will still live in extreme poverty in 2015.

⇨ Progress is less encouraging at higher poverty lines. Only a modest drop in the number of people living below $2 per day – the average poverty line for developing countries – occurred between 1981 and 2008, from 2.59 to 2.47 billion. With 1.18 billion people living on $1.25 to $2 per day in 2008, a great many people remain vulnerable and poor by standards of middle-income developing countries.

Poverty: recent estimates and outlook

In every region of the developing world, both the percentage and number of people living on less than $1.25 a day declined between 2005 and 2008. This across-the-board reduction over a three-year monitoring cycle marks a first since the Bank began monitoring extreme poverty.

In 2008, 1.29 billion people lived below $1.25 a day, equivalent to 22 per cent of the population in the developing world. Nearly three quarters of this total resided in South Asia (571 million) and Sub-Saharan Africa (396 million). Another 284 million lived in East Asia, and less than 50 million in Latin America and the Caribbean, Middle East and North Africa, and Eastern Europe and Central Asia combined. By contrast, in 1981, 1.94 billion people (52 per cent of the population) were living in extreme poverty.

While poverty has declined in all regions, progress has been uneven. East Asia exhibited the most dramatic reduction, slashing its $1.25 a day poverty rate from 77 per cent in 1981 to 14 percent in 2008. In South Asia, the proportion of the population living in extreme poverty is now the lowest it has been since 1981, falling from 61 to 36 percent between 1981 and 2008. Sub-Saharan Africa reduced the $1.25 a day poverty rate to 47 percent in 2008 – the first time it has dipped below 50 percent. Also, the number of the extreme poor in the region declined since 2005, reversing the long-run increase

from about 200 million in 1981 to almost 400 million in 2005.

Although China alone accounted for 663 million fewer people living on less than $1.25 a day in 2008 than 1981, around the time the country's reform period began, the $1.25 a day poverty rate for the rest of the developing world (without China) still fell from 41 to 25 per cent between 1981 and 2008. On the other hand, due to population growth the total poverty count (without China) was around 1.1 billion people in both 1981 and 2008, although the number had risen and fallen in between these years.

Other poverty lines show similar trends. A higher standard like the $2 per day poverty line is more appropriate for more developed regions. Over the period as a whole, the $2 a day poverty rate declined from 70 to 43 per cent, but the number of people living below this line only dropped from 2.59 to 2.47 billion. The number has risen and then fallen substantially since 1999, when 2.94 billion lived below $2 a day.

How the World Bank is fighting poverty

At the heart of the Bank's work is its focus on poverty reduction and improving opportunities for the poor. In addition to causing hunger and malnutrition, poverty makes people vulnerable to shocks, such as the global economic crisis, climate change and natural disasters. The World Bank seeks to reduce poverty by supporting the design and implementation of country poverty-reduction strategies through a variety of analytical and lending instruments. It aims to expand growth opportunities, reduce vulnerability to shocks, and improve poor people's access to basic services.

Despite the global economic crisis and other shocks, preliminary estimates for 2010 indicate that poverty continued to fall and that the first MDG goal was met. However, it remains that 1.2 billion people still live in extreme poverty, as judged by the $1.25 a day line, and nearly two and half billion people live on less than $2 a day. Clearly, the Bank has more to do in its fight against poverty. With global growth prospects recently downgraded and downside risks still on the horizon, challenges loom for developing countries. In light of these challenges and implications for poverty, the Bank is focused on creating more and better jobs, delivering better educational and health services and basic infrastructure, and protecting vulnerable groups.

Country-led development strategies

Many developing countries have prepared national strategies to boost their effort to combat poverty. They define clear national plans and priorities for achieving fighting poverty, linking policy agendas to medium-term fiscal frameworks. As of February 2012, 67 low– and lower–middle–income countries prepared Poverty Reduction Strategy Papers (PRSPs) and 37 of them already produced the second or third generation of PRSPs. Also, many middle income countries set poverty reduction as targets or included different dimensions of poverty in their development objectives. The Bank aligns its activities to these national strategies through its Country Assistance Strategies or Country Partnership Strategies, which serve as a basis for harmonization with other development partners.

Useful links

⇨ For more information on poverty, see: www.worldbank.org/poverty.

⇨ For poverty data, see: http://povertydata.worldbank.org and http://econ.worldbank.org/povcalnet.

⇨ For the latest World Bank poverty research, see: http://econ.worldbank.org/programs/poverty.

March 2012

⇨ The above information is reprinted with kind permission from The World Bank Group. Visit www.worldbank.org for further information.

Regional highlights

East Asia and the Pacific

About 14 per cent of its population lived below US$1.25 a day in 2008, down from 77 per cent in 1981, when it was the region with the highest poverty rate in the world. In China, 13 per cent, or 173 million people, lived below $1.25 a day in 2008. East Asia achieved MDG1 about ten years ago.

In the developing world outside China, the extreme-poverty rate was 25 per cent in 2008, down from 41 per cent in 1981. The number of people living in extreme poverty, however, was about the same in 2008 as 1981 at around 1.1 billion, after rising in the 1980s and 1990s and falling since 1999.

South Asia

The $1.25 a day poverty rate fell from 61 per cent to 39 per cent between 1981 and 2005 and fell a further three percentage points between 2005 and 2008. The proportion of the population living in extreme poverty is now the lowest since 1981.

Latin America and the Caribbean

From a peak of 14 per cent living below $1.25 a day in 1984, the poverty rate reached its lowest value so far of 6.5 per cent in 2008. The number of the poor rose until 2002 and has been falling sharply since.

Middle East and North Africa

The region had 8.6 million people – or 2.7 per cent of the population – living on less than $1.25 a day in 2008, down from 10.5 million in 2005 and 16.5 million in 1981.

Eastern Europe and Central Asia

The proportion living on less than $1.25 is now under 0.5 per cent, having peaked at 3.8 per cent in 1999. 2.2 per cent lived on less than $2 a day in 2008, down from a peak of 12 per cent in 1999.

Sub-Saharan Africa

For the first time since 1981, less than half of its population (47 percent) lived below $1.25 a day. The rate was 51 per cent in 1981. The $1.25-a-day poverty rate in SSA has fallen ten percentage points since 1999. nine million fewer people are living below $1.25 a day in 2008 than 2005.

29 February 2012

⇨ The above information is reprinted with kind permission from The World Bank Group. Visit www.worldbank.org for further information.

Eradicating extreme poverty and hunger

***Extract from* The Millenium Development Goals Report, 2011.**

TARGET: Halve, between 1990 and 2015, the proportion of people whose income is less than $1 a day

Sustained growth in developing countries, particularly in Asia, is keeping the world on track to meet the poverty-reduction target

Robust growth in the first half of the decade reduced the number of people in developing countries living on less than $1.25 a day from about 1.8 billion in 1990 to 1.4 billion in 2005. At the same time, the corresponding poverty rate dropped from 46 per cent to 27 per cent. The economic and financial crisis that began in the advanced countries of North America and Europe in 2008 sparked declines in commodity prices, trade and investment, resulting in slower growth globally.

Despite these declines, current trends suggest that the movement of growth in the developing world remains strong enough to sustain progress needed to reach the global poverty-reduction target. Based on recently updated projections from the World Bank, the overall poverty rate is still expected to fall below 15 per cent by 2015, indicating that the Millenium Development Goal (MDG) target can be met.

The World Bank's new poverty projections for 2015 incorporate several changes: additional data from over 60 new household surveys, updates of historical consumption per capita from national accounts, and a new forecast of growth in per capita consumption. The forecast therefore captures changes in income distribution in countries for which new survey data

are available, and assumes that inequality remains unchanged in other countries. It also incorporates some of the effects of the global economic crisis, such as food and fuel price shocks. By 2015, the number of people in developing countries living on less than $1.25 a day is projected to fall below 900 million.

The fastest growth and sharpest reductions in poverty continue to be found in Eastern Asia, particularly in China, where the poverty rate is expected to fall to under five per cent by 2015. India has also contributed to the large reduction in global poverty. In that country, poverty rates are projected to fall from 51 per cent in 1990 to about 22 per cent in 2015. In China and India combined, the number of people living in extreme poverty between 1990 and 2005 declined by about 455 million, and an additional 320 million people are expected to join their ranks by 2015. Projections for Sub-Saharan Africa are slightly more upbeat than previously estimated. Based on recent economic growth performance and forecasted trends, the extreme poverty rate in the region is expected to fall below 36 per cent.

The task of monitoring progress on poverty reduction is beset by a lack of good quality surveys carried out at regular intervals, delays in reporting survey results, and insufficient documentation of country level analytical methods used. It is also hampered by difficulties in accessing the underlying survey microdata required to compute the poverty estimates. These gaps remain particularly problematic in Sub-Saharan Africa, where the data necessary to make comparisons over the full range of MDGs are available in less than half the countries. For example, between 2007 and 2009, the countries that had collected, analysed and disseminated survey data, represent only 20 per cent of the region's population.

TARGET: Achieve full and productive employment and decent work for all, including women and young people

Economic recovery has failed to translate into employment opportunities

More than three years have passed since the onset of the fastest and deepest drop in global economic activity since the Great Depression. While global economic growth is rebounding, the global labour market is, in many respects, behaving as anticipated in the middle of the crisis: stubbornly elevated unemployment and slow employment generation in developed economies, coupled with widespread deficits in decent work in even the fastest-growing developing countries.

In the developed regions, the employment–to–population ratio dropped from 56.8 per cent in 2007 to 55.4 per cent in 2009, with a further drop to 54.8 per cent in 2010. Clearly, many developed economies are simply not generating sufficient employment opportunities to absorb growth in the working-age population. Again, this reflects an ongoing lag between economic recovery and a recovery in employment in this region. This contrasts with many developing regions, some of which saw an initial decline in the employment-to-population ratio but where, with the exception of the Caucasus and Central Asia and Eastern Asia, the estimated employment-to-population ratio in 2010 has changed little since 2007.

Progress in reducing vulnerable employment stalled following the economic crisis

In developing regions overall, the majority of workers are engaged in 'vulnerable employment', defined as the percentage of own-account and unpaid family workers in total employment. Vulnerable employment is characterised by informal working arrangements, lack of adequate social protection, low pay and difficult working conditions.

On the basis of available data, it is estimated that the vulnerable employment rate remained roughly the same between 2008 and 2009, both in developing and developed regions. This compares with a steady average decline in the years preceding the economic and financial crisis. Increases in the vulnerable employment rate were found in Sub-Saharan Africa and Western Asia.

A slowdown in progress against poverty is reflected in the number of working poor. According to the International Labour Organization, one in five workers and their families worldwide were living in extreme poverty (on less than $1.25 per person per day) in 2009. This represents a sharp decline in poverty from a decade earlier, but also a flattening of the slope of the working poverty incidence curve beginning in 2007.

The estimated rate for 2009 is 1.6 percentage points higher than the rate projected on the basis of the pre-crisis trend. While this is a crude estimate, it amounts to about 40 million more working poor at the extreme $1.25 level in 2009 than would have been expected on the basis of pre-crisis trends.

TARGET: Halve, between 1990 and 2005, the proportion of people who suffer from hunger

The proportion of people going hungry has plateaued at 16 per cent, despite reductions in poverty

The proportion of people in the developing world who went hungry in 2005–2007 remained stable at 16 per cent, despite significant reductions in extreme poverty. Based on this trend, and in light of the economic crisis and rising food prices, it will be difficult to meet the hunger-reduction target in many regions of the developing world.

The disconnect between poverty reduction and the persistence of hunger has brought renewed attention to the mechanisms governing access to food in the developing world. This year, the Food and Agriculture Organization of the United Nations will undertake a comprehensive review of the causes behind this apparent discrepancy to better inform hunger-reduction policies in the future.

Disparities within and among regions are found in the fight against hunger

Trends observed in South-Eastern Asia, Eastern Asia and Latin America and the Caribbean suggest that they are likely to meet the hunger-reduction target by 2015. However, wide disparities are found among countries in these regions. For example, the strong gains recorded in Eastern Asia since 1990 are largely due to progress in China, while levels in South-Eastern Asia benefit from advances made in Indonesia and the Philippines. Based on current trends, Sub-Saharan Africa will be unable to meet the hunger-reduction target by 2015.

Nearly a quarter of children in the developing world remain undernourished

In developing regions, the proportion of children under age five who are underweight declined from 30 per cent to 23 per cent between 1990 and 2009. Progress in reducing underweight prevalence was made in all regions where comparable trend data are available. Eastern Asia, Latin America and the Caribbean, and the Caucasus and Central Asia have reached or nearly reached the MDG target, and South-Eastern Asia and Northern Africa are on track.

However, progress in the developing regions overall is insufficient to reach the target by 2015. Children are underweight due to a combination of factors: lack of quality food, suboptimal feeding practices, repeated attacks of infectious diseases and pervasive undernutrition. In Southern Asia, for example, one finds not only a shortage of quality food and poor feeding practices, but a lack of flush toilets and other forms of improved sanitation. Nearly half the population practises open defecation, resulting in repeated bouts of diarrhoeal disease in children, which contribute to the high prevalence of undernutrition. Moreover, more than a quarter of infants in that region weigh less than 2,500 grams at birth. Many of these children are never able to catch up in terms of their nutritional status. All these factors conspire to make underweight prevalence in the region the highest in the world.

Nutrition must be given higher priority in national development if the MDGs are to be achieved. A number of simple, cost-effective measures delivered at key stages of the life cycle, particularly from conception to two years after birth, could greatly reduce undernutrition. These measures include improved maternal nutrition and care, breastfeeding within one hour of birth, exclusive breastfeeding for the first six months of life, and timely, adequate, safe, and appropriate complementary feeding and micronutrient intake between six and 24 months of age. Urgent, accelerated and concerted actions are needed to deliver and scale up such interventions to achieve MDG1 and other health-related goals.

In Southern Asia, progress in combating child undernutrition is bypassing the poorest

Children from the poorest households are more likely to be underweight than their richer counterparts. Moreover, the poorest children are making the slowest progress in reducing underweight prevalence. In Southern Asia, for example, there was no meaningful improvement among children in the poorest households in the period between 1995 and 2009, while underweight prevalence among children from the richest 20 per cent of households decreased by almost a third.

Children in developing regions are twice as likely to be underweight if they live in rural rather than urban areas. Little difference was found in underweight prevalence between girls and boys.

Close to 43 million people worldwide are displaced because of conflict or persecution

Humanitarian crises and conflicts continue to uproot millions of people across the globe. They also hinder the return of refugees and those internally displaced. As of end 2010,

close to 43 million people worldwide were displaced due to conflict and persecution, the highest number since the mid-1990s and about half a million more than the previous year. Of these, 15.4 million are refugees, including 10.5 million who fall under the responsibility of the United Nations High Commissioner for Refugees (UNHCR) and 4.8 million Palestinian refugees who are the responsibility of the United Nations Relief and Works Agency for Palestine Refugees in the Near East (UNRWA). In addition, 27.5 million people have been uprooted by violence and persecution but remain within the borders of their own countries. While often not displaced per se, UNHCR estimated that some 12 million people were stateless. While millions of refugees have found a durable solution to their situation over the decades, others have been confined to camps and other settlements for many years without any solution in sight. Excluding refugees under UNRWA's mandate, UNHCR estimates that 7.2 million refugees spread across 24 countries are currently trapped in a protracted situation of this kind. This is the highest number since 2001 and clearly demonstrates the lack of permanent solutions for many of the world's refugees. The number of refugees who have returned to their homes has continuously decreased since 2004, with the 2010 figures (197,600 returns) being the lowest since 1990.

On average, four out of five refugees are hosted by developing countries. Afghans and Iraqis continue to be the largest refugee populations under the UNHCR mandate with three million and 1.7 million refugees, respectively, at the end of 2010. Together they account for nearly half of all refugees under UNHCR's mandate.

⇨ Extract from The Millenium Development Goals Report 2011. Reprinted with kind permission from United Nations. Visit www.un.org for further information.

© United Nations, 2011

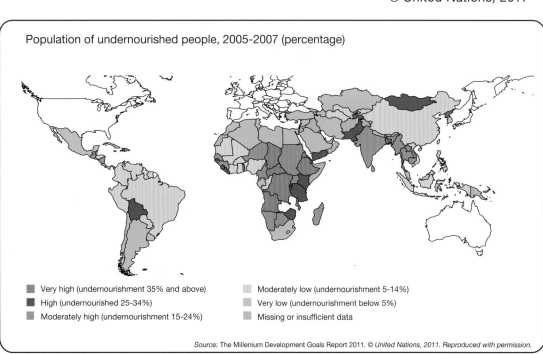

Population of undernourished people, 2005-2007 (percentage)

- ■ Very high (undernourishment 35% and above)
- ■ High (undernourished 25-34%)
- ■ Moderately high (undernourishment 15-24%)
- ■ Moderately low (undernourishment 5-14%)
- ■ Very low (undernourishment below 5%)
- ■ Missing or insufficient data

Source: The Millenium Development Goals Report 2011. © United Nations, 2011. Reproduced with permission.

The new 'bottom billion'

What if 72 per cent of the world's poor don't live in poor countries? Andy Sumner of the Institute of Development Studies outlines the findings of his latest research.

The global poverty problem has changed. In the past, poor people lived in poor countries but now there are around 960 million poor people, or a 'new bottom billion', living on under $1.25/day in middle-income countries, and most of these are in stable, non-fragile, middle-income countries.

Redefining the 'bottom billion'

This new bottom billion accounts for 72 per cent – almost three-quarters – of the world's poor. Only about a quarter of the world's poor – 370 million people or so – live in the remaining 39 low-income countries, which are largely in Sub-Saharan Africa.

These findings are similar across nutrition indicators and the UN Development Programme's new multidimensional poverty index. The exception is in education where 60 per cent of children out of primary school are in low-income countries compared to just 40 per cent in middle-income countries.

This is a dramatic change from just two decades ago when 93 per cent of poor people lived in low-income countries. This change

Paul Collier's bottom billion

In 2007, Collier published a book titled *The Bottom Billion: Why the Poorest Countries are Failing and What Can Be Done About It*. In this book, Collier defines the 'bottom billion' as the world's 60 poorest countries, that are home to about a billion people. This implied that, if you lived in one of these countries, you were poor.

has major implications for both the achievement of the Millennium Development Goals and global strategies for poverty reduction beyond 2015.

In fact, the change raises questions for donors, governments in middle-income countries, NGOs in North and South and researchers. There is a real prospect of ending poverty by 2025 because the resources exist to do it. How does this new geography of global poverty change things?

The poor live in three types of places:

⇨ Low-income countries – one quarter of the world's poor

⇨ Middle-income countries – three quarters of the world's poor

⇨ Fragile/conflict-affected states – these are a mix of low– and middle–income countries and represent around a quarter which overlaps the above.

Which countries do we mean?

Democratic Republic of Congo and Burundi are low-income countries that are also fragile/conflict-affected states, while stable low-income countries include Zambia and Tanzania. Pakistan and Nigeria are both middle-income countries that are fragile/conflict-affected, whereas stable middle-income countries are India and Indonesia.

Why has it taken so long to realise we were getting it wrong?

Good data runs two to three years late at least and the numbers reflect a long run pattern that became particularly visible over last year or so as a number of countries reached middle-income status.

Don't the poor or 'bottom billion' live in fragile states? About one

in four or five do. Paul Collier's bottom billion were always the billion people not the billion poor people living in 58 countries that were 'falling apart or falling behind'. Collier's assumption is that poverty is 100 per cent in these countries. In the IDS estimates, total fragile/conflict-affected low- and middle-income countries account for about 23 per cent, or about 300 million or so.

Taking Collier's approach

When we looked more closely at Collier's 58 countries, we found that we have reasonably good poverty data coverage for those countries. Collier's 58 bottom billion countries represent:

⇨ close to a billion people in total population but only 27 per cent of the world's poor

⇨ around 30 per cent of undernourished children

⇨ around 30 per cent of the poor according to the new UNDP multidimensional poverty measure.

Collier's 58 countries also have a high proportion of the global out of primary school children (57 per cent).

Things have changed too. A third, or 300 million, of the total population of Collier's 58 bottom billion countries now live in World Bank-classified middle-income countries and one in five of the total population of Collier's 58 bottom billion countries no longer live in fragile/conflict-affected states if they ever did (we used the broadest possible definition – 43 countries – by combining the three fragile/conflict-affected states lists).

What does this all mean?

Collier's approach is out of date and overlooks around 70 per cent of the poor people in the world. If development is primarily about fighting poverty, that is a lot.

This doesn't invalidate Collier's key point: that the poor in his bottom billion 58 countries (even if only are 27 per cent of the total world's poor) are trapped and without hope so development needs to focus there; it simply means we would raise a question mark over his assumption that there is no need to worry about the other 70 per cent or the 'new bottom billion' because growth will look after them.

The second assumption he makes is also questionable – that the donor community is able to contribute positively to springing these traps in his 58 countries. It is not clear what the evidence is for this.

Poor people haven't moved of course. What has happened is the countries many poor people live in have got richer – attained middle-income country status – and the data suggests that they have been left behind.

So, what if the poor live in countries that have got richer, why does it matter?

It matters because it raises a lot of questions about aid and development policy 'beyond aid'. If development is about poverty reduction, where poor people live is a crucial question.

How should donors, policy makers, NGOs and practitioners respond to the 'new bottom billion'?

⇨ The above information is reprinted with kind permission from Bond Overseas Non-Governmental Organisations for Development. Visit www. bond.org.uk for further information on this and other subjects.

© Bond 2012

How 28 poor countries escaped the poverty trap

Zambia and Ghana are the 27th and 28th countries The World Bank has reclassified as middle-income since the year 2000.

By Charles Kenny and Andy Sumner

Remember the poverty trap? Countries stuck in destitution because of weak institutions put in place by colonial overlords, or because of climates that foster disease, or geographies that limit access to global markets, or simply by the fact that poverty is overwhelmingly self-perpetuating. Apparently the trap can be escaped.

The World Bank did its annual assessment of poor countries last week. Low-income countries are those with average gross national incomes (GNIs) of less than $1,005 per person per year.

And there are only 35 of them remaining out of the countries and economies that The World Bank tracks. That's down from 63 in 2000.

New middle-income countries this year include Ghana and Zambia. Lower-middle-income countries are those with per capita GNIs of between $1,006 and $3,975 per year; while upper-middle-income countries are those with per capita GNIs between $3,976 and $12,275.

The remaining 35 low-income countries have a combined population of about 800 million. Tanzania, Burma, the Democratic Republic of the Congo, Ethiopia and Bangladesh account for about half of that total, and there are about 350 million people living on under $1.25 a day in the remaining low-income countries.

So what's behind all of this sudden income growth? Is it a story about aid? One prominent Zambian, Dambisa Moyo, has written of her country that 'a direct consequence of the aid-driven interventions has been a dramatic descent into poverty. Whereas prior to the 1970s, most economic indicators had been on an upward trajectory, a decade later Zambia lay in economic ruin'. In the 1980s, aid to Zambia averaged about 14% of the country's GNI. In the 2000s, a decade of strong growth, the same proportion was 17%. If Zambia's ruin in the 1980s was the result of aid, is Zambia's graduation to middle-income status in the new millennium a sign that aid now works really well?

Of course both the ideas that previous stagnation was all the fault of aid, or current growth was all the result, are ridiculous. The price of copper (Zambia's major export) was depressed in the 1980s and saw its price rocket in the middle of the last decade as China and India's economies grew and demand for the metal soared.

But growth among low-income countries in Africa and elsewhere isn't just limited to big mineral exporters. And the continent is fast drawing in more investment. Foreign direct investment to Africa is projected to rise to $150 billion by 2015, reports the *Africa Attractiveness Survey* (that's more than the total global aid budget) – and domestic resources are being mobilised at a faster rate, too, as the Commission for Africa 2010 report discussed.

Even gold and diamond-producing Ghana, which declared itself 63% richer at the end of last year than previously thought, didn't suggest the new-found riches were the result of mineral exports. Instead, the recalculation was driven by the fact the country's services sector was a lot bigger than previously calculated. Part of that will reflect the incredible success of the telecoms sector – 75% of the country's population are mobile subscribers. And, of course, the expansion of telecoms is a worldwide phenomenon. So a lot of the growth we are seeing in poor countries is broad-based, not just reliant on the current commodity boom – which is good news for the future.

Of course there's much to do to translate this growth into better and faster poverty reduction. Looking at the progress data for the Millennium Development Goals (MDGs) for Ghana and Zambia there's nowhere near the kind of progress you would hope to see on income poverty. 20 years of growth in Ghana has reduced the number of people living on $1.25 or less from just over seven million to just under seven million – and inequality (as measured by the Gini coefficient) rose significantly. However, in both Ghana and Zambia, the number of children in primary school has climbed along with literacy rates, and infant mortality has fallen. Even if they're not on track to meet the MDGs, quality of life is getting much better.

What shall we take from this? Three things. First, consider the good news that there are fewer poor countries around. Not least, it suggests that public and private investment (including aid) can help even the poorest countries get rich(er). This is one more reason why optimism should come back into fashion.

Second, The World Bank country classifications – which are used to help determine types and levels of support provided by many aid agencies – may need a rethink. They are based on a decades-old formula, and on the idea that most poor people live in poor countries. But we know that middle-income countries now account for most of the world's population living in absolute poverty. And the data suggests these aren't just poor countries by another name – they really are better off than low-income countries, not only in terms of average income but by human development and other development indicators too. We need aid allocation models to take account of poor people and of deprivations beyond income – not just poor countries with a low GNI. And fewer poor countries and poor people in time also suggests greater aid funds for global public goods - be these for climate adaptation, vaccines or other shared global issues that will shape the next 25 years.

Third, as countries develop their own resources, fighting poverty becomes increasingly about domestic politics. Not surprisingly, this means inequality is rising up the agenda. New research shows that the emerging middle classes may have a big role to play.

Who they side with – the poorest or the economic elite – will determine what kind of development emerges in the new middle-income countries.

In short, even the poorest countries can get richer – and that's a good news story.

⇨ Charles Kenny is a research fellow at the Center for Global Development and the author of *Getting Better: Why Global Development Is Succeeding - And How We Can Improve the World Even More.*

⇨ Andy Sumner is a research fellow at the Institute of Development Studies and a visiting fellow at the Center for Global Development.

12 July 2011

⇨ The above article originally appeared in the *Guardian.* Please visit www.guardian.co.uk for more information.

© *Guardian News & Media Ltd. 2012*

Population living on under US$1.25 pc/day (m)

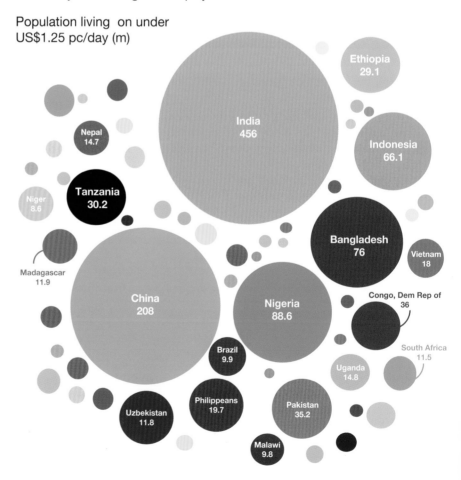

Source: Which bottom billion? Poverty indicators. *The Guardian.14 September 2010.*
© *Guardian News & Media Ltd. 2012*

Debate report: Britain must cut its overseas aid budget now

*Lloyd Evans reviews **The Spectator's** debate on whether Britain should cut its overseas aid budget.*

Chair: Rod Liddle

Proposing: Ian Birrell, Richard Dowden, Stephen Glover

Opposing: Prof. Paul Collier, Alan Duncan MP, Richard Miller

Ian Birrell, former speechwriter for David Cameron, proposed the motion by likening aid programmes to helping child beggars in the third world. The gift, though well-intentioned, keeps children out of school, encourages more kids to start begging and condemns entire families to penury. If aid worked, Birrell would happily treble it. But it distorts economies and humiliates the recipients. 'Aid workers are the new colonials, driving around in 4x4s and earning many times more than locals.' Waste is inevitable. Barely 40p in every pound, he said, reaches the intended beneficiaries. And aid promotes corruption. Uganda's president spent $30 million on a new jet three years ago – equivalent to half his country's annual aid budget. And aid encourages tyranny. Rwanda, which receives huge chunks of UK cash, has been accused of sending hit-squads to Britain to assassinate its government's enemies. David Cameron's commitment to spend 0.7 per cent of GDP on foreign aid is an arbitrary target based on out-moded statistics. And though aid makes us feel good, it leaves a chaotic legacy. Aid promotes Africa as a 'helpless supplicant in need of help from heroes in the west'. Images of poverty and crisis deter westerners from engaging in trade, and in tourism, which could deliver long-term prosperity. Aid mustn't be confused with development. Birrell pointed to Somaliland, an autonomous region of Somalia, which manages to feed itself and which has a relatively stable democracy. It receives no aid.

Paul Collier, director of the Centre for the Study of African Economics at Oxford, attacked the 'squalid' motion as an attempt to vindicate heartless parsimony. 'Just because we're hard up we're going to cut money for the poor.' He warned against overestimating our importance in the third world. 'Africa is a struggle between Africans. We're the supporting cast.' Aid alone, he said, cannot destroy a society because, 'societies make or destroy themselves'. Responsibly administered aid can be an instrument of good governance. And the UK aid programme is 'a world-beater' which gives our demoralised youth something to be proud of. Aid is more than a sign of our moral worth, it's 'a chance to be magnificent and Quixotic'. To vote against the motion would be to break a government pledge. 'Where would your pride be,' he asked, 'and your sense of shame?'

Richard Dowden, commentator on African affairs, differentiated emergency relief programmes, which he supports, from aid programmes which merely offer us 'a feel-good fig-leaf'. Africa is a poor country, run by rich elites, and 'aid keeps them in power'. African governments research western aid programmes scrupulously. And they aren't constrained by targets or by public opinion. 'They know us better than we know them.' Once we start to donate, 'we're trapped'. Dowden reckons that with rising African prosperity, driven by Chinese investment, aid will become less relevant. 'They're not as dependent on us any more.' Africa's real problem was 'capital flight'. So instead of focusing on aid, we should attempt to prevent the huge outflows of wealth from Africa. We need to reform our visa system too. Ethiopians have to travel to Nairobi to gain a UK entry permit.

Alan Duncan, Minister of State at DfID, confessed that he once believed overseas aid should be privatised. He now regards it as the foundation of our claim to be a civilised society. Public opposition, he said, was 'skin deep' and based on a misconception that aid absorbs as much as a quarter of Britain's income. Relative to GDP, the budget is miniscule. 'Even if you were down to your last hundred quid, would you refuse to give a dying man 50p?' He praised his department's recent reforms and its new focus on results, on value for money, and on external scrutiny. 'Transparency is a god. You can see on the website how every penny is spent.' Duncan recognised that aid involves 'imperfect and mucky countries' but he distinguished governments from people. 'Bad governance doesn't mean we shouldn't help the poorest in those countries.' And he preferred to talk of

'development' rather than 'dependency'. Aid means lifting people out of poverty and helping them sustain their own livelihoods.

Stephen Glover, columnist for the *Daily Mail,* argued that opponents of aid shouldn't be cast as 'morally defective, or beastly people'. The motion specified the word 'cut', which didn't mean outright abolition. He found it 'impossible to accept intellectually' that the aid budget had to be ring-fenced at a time when most other departments were trimming costs. He objected to the waste and corruption aid brings. 'It's childish to pretend large amounts aren't being creamed off.' Britain's donation to Pakistan is set to rise from £140 million to £350 million and yet Imran Khan has stated that 'little aid reaches the intended recipients'. And Glover pointed to India, the biggest single beneficiary of Britain's largesse, whose economy is, by certain measures, already larger than ours. Cameron's pledge to protect the aid programme was a PR stunt intended to 'detoxify the nasty party'. The Government should have the humility to think again.

Richard Miller, a director of ActionAid UK, offered a simple message: aid works. Medical programmes undertaken since 1990 mean that 10,000 fewer children die of preventable diseases every day. 'That's 60 lives saved,' he said, 'during the nine minutes I'm speaking to you.' In 1983 he visited crisis-torn Ghana where the demoralised citizens regarded emigration as their only hope. By 2010, Ghana had been transformed. 'The numbers going hungry have fallen by 75 per cent, and eight of ten Ghanaian children attend school.' Stable government and a sense of optimism have brought the emigrants back. In Rwanda, a British aid programme in 2000 reformed the revenue system and introduced 'tax justice'. The Rwandan Government is now able spend its own income on its own initiatives. Miller reminded us that many third world countries plan to end their aid programmes altogether. 'We shouldn't waste our investment now by cutting aid.' It's unacceptable, 'to turn our backs on malnourished babies and mothers for whom childbirth is Russian roulette'.

The motion was defeated.

3 November 2011

⇨ Information from *The Spectator.* Visit www.spectator. co.uk for further information.

Definitions of aid

International aid for poorer countries.

1. Government aid

Most international aid has come as direct loan or grant aid from one government to another government, with richer governments like the US often being the bigger aid givers. But this aid has generally gone to 'friendly' governments, rather than to the countries in greater need. And it has often been military aid.

2. International Body aid

Other international direct loan or grant aid has come from two bodies established in the 1940s, the World Bank and the International Monetary Fund (IMF). The World Bank has been the bigger donor of both aid loans and aid grants chiefly for redevelopment or reconstruction, while the IMF has mainly managed exchange rates and gives some aid loans. Both of these bodies have been substantially under US Government control and of limited effect in reducing world poverty, but these bodies have recently been concentrating on increasing aid predictability to improve aid effectiveness.

3. Charity aid

Charities of many kinds also give some aid in various forms, more often emergency or crisis aid but also a little longer-term aid.

Most of the little international aid going to poorer countries has been ineffective in reducing poverty in the longer term, though there have been a few real success cases.

Aid for the poor in richer countries.

1. Government aid

Most aid for the poor in richer countries has come from their government, some in the form of universal benefits but more as means-tested benefits. But this poor aid has generally gone more to those viewed as 'deserving' poor, rather than to those in greater need. Some also involves non-poverty policy aims, such as recent UK Government trials of free school meals. And poverty aid has often been aid of limited longer-term use.

2. Charity aid

Some richer-country charities also give some aid in various forms to some of their poor, more often emergency or crisis aid but also some longer-term aid as well. This aid is generally very limited and often also less effective than it could be.

With around 80 million estimated to be living in relative poverty in the EU, the European Union has made 2010 the European Year For Combating Poverty and Social Exclusion. There will be conferences and other events to raise public awareness, but as yet no new commitment to action by their governments.

In richer countries, trying to target their poor people can create so many problems that often poor people can be helped more by targeting them less.

⇨ Information from World Poverty. Please visit www. world-poverty.org for further information.

Britain to kick start banking for the poorest

The UK Government will unlock the potential of entrepreneurs in the poorest countries and create almost one million new jobs.

Speaking at the World Bank in Washington DC, Secretary of State for International Development Andrew Mitchell will set out how Britain and the International Finance Corporation (IFC) will help banks provide much-needed capital to promising businesses.

A new global small and medium-sized enterprise (SME) finance facility will be created to help nearly a quarter of a million businesses access capital over the next seven years, with at least a quarter of these loans for organisations headed by women.

'Small and medium enterprises are a vital engine of job creation in developing countries'

Working with commercial banks, the fund will focus assistance on some of the poorest and most fragile countries in Africa and South Asia, such as South Sudan, Malawi, Liberia, Uganda, Mozambique, Sierra Leone, Bangladesh and Nepal.

Secretary of State for International Development, Andrew Mitchell, said:

'Entrepreneurs don't want handouts. They want opportunities to help them pull themselves out of poverty. They need investment to build their businesses and create stable jobs. Using expert banking knowledge and new technology we will be able to kick start the engine of growth.'

'We have no chance of defeating global poverty unless we unblock commercial lending and allow entrepreneurs the chance to thrive in some of the most neglected parts of the world.'

Lars Thunell, IFC Executive Vice-President and CEO, said:

"Small and medium enterprises are a vital engine of job creation in developing countries. Yet they face a huge financing gap – especially in Africa, where SMEs need three times more funding than is currently available. This facility will help narrow the gap, creating opportunity for entrepreneurs who need it most."

Many banks are often unable to fully assess the risks of investing, greatly overestimating the cost of a loan. For example, fees for lending were almost three times as high in developing countries compared to rich countries.

The new facility will share innovative technology and expert banking knowledge to strengthen the skills, systems and processes.

This will include:

⇨ Unlocking the supply capital from banks in poor countries to free-up an additional £5 billion of private sector lending to small and medium-sized enterprises. A small start-up pool of capital will help 35 private banks and institutions to spread the risk of investing and reduce their transaction costs.

⇨ Fast-financing will see direct lending to SMEs in poor countries.

⇨ Bringing in innovative technology to speed up lending and reduce risk. State of the art psychometric credit scoring tests which help banks predict the risk and potential of business ideas and borrowers.

⇨ Setting up modern banking techniques to reduce the risk of lending. This will bring down the cost of lending to promising small businesses.

'Entrepreneurs don't want handouts. They want opportunities to help them pull themselves out of poverty'

SMEs already employ two thirds of the total permanent work force in developing countries, but less than one third of all small businesses in Pakistan, Bangladesh and DRC have any deposit or credit account with banks. Being able to access finance will enable businesses to generate more jobs and help create a more prosperous and peaceful future.

22 April 2012

⇨ Information from the Department for International Development. Please visit www.dfid.gov.uk.

Ten amazing microfinance success stories

Information from MBA News.

The benefits of microfinance have been debated since the '70s when the Grameen Bank in Bangladesh began making tiny loans to impoverished small business owners. In 2006, Muhammad Yunus, the bank's founder and 'the father of microfinance', won the Nobel Peace Prize. Since that time, at least one study has shown the practice does little to empower women in oppressed cultures or improve quality of life for poor people. Yet there are still those who point to amazing microfinance success stories like these as proof that conscious lending can be a good deal for more than just the money men.

1. Reuben Mpunda, Tanzania

Mpunda had struggled for ten years working at a hotel, a brewery, and a ruby mine. When he hit on the idea of selling clean water, a scarce commodity in Africa, he could barely afford the fees to power his tank. After three years of scraping by, he borrowed half a million Tanzanian shillings (or $360) from the Akiba Commercial Bank. The money helped him pay the municipal fees and buy three trucks to deliver water. His output shot up over 1,100% and his profits increased nearly six-fold. He's using the money to buy more nutritious food for his family and pay for his sons' schooling.

2. Macelino Lopez, Colombia

Lopez and his family were living in a plastic tent in Barrio Nelson Mandela, Colombia, with $300 to his name. Driven to a refugee camp by guerrilla violence, Lopez turned to Fundación Mario Santo Domingo for a $95 loan and opened a small convenience store. A year later, Lopez had moved his family into a concrete home where he ran the most successful butcher shop in the barrio.

3. Nadya Fleah, Jordan

The Microfund For Women helped transform Nadya Felah from a janitor into a successful businesswoman. She started a business selling gas cylinders with a loan from MFW that helped her buy two cars to make deliveries. In two years she has hired eight full-time employees, secured lucrative government contracts, and is able to support seven households besides her own in Amman. She is even mulling a run for office in the gas providers' union.

4. Lidia Calzado, U.S.

Not all microfinance stories take place in remote villages in Third World countries. Lidia Calzado received a $10,000 loan from ACCION San Diego that allowed her to buy more inventory and thereby circumvent her supplier's high interest rate. Her business selling jewellery and perfume is still growing, enough that Calzado can afford to do charity work with immigrant women. Amazingly, Calzado herself emigrated to the U.S. from Cuba despite speaking no English and being legally blind.

5. SHARE Micro Finance Limited, India

Since its organisation in 1999, SHARE has become the biggest microfinance institution in India, and its success has prompted other banks to begin their own microfinance programmes. The bank lends to groups of women, with each receiving $50 to $100 to buy rickshaws for transporting wheat to market or to help them open Internet kiosks. Of nearly 200,000 clients, over 98% of whom are female, 77% have significantly raised their income level away from poverty, and 38% no longer fall below the poverty line.

6. Joyce Wafukho, Kenya

Joyce Wafukho used her small savings to open a hardware store in 1994. But with insufficient capital, she was able to sell only a few items. After five years of being turned down by lenders, she approached the Kenya Women Finance Trust for a $680 loan. Today, after five more loans from KWFT, Wafukho employs 25 Africans full-time in her business, which now also includes contracting and selling lumber. The business has assets of $27,000 and Wafukho is able to pay for not only her children's health and education, but for her sister to go to college for a master's degree.

7. Parveen Baji, Pakistan

All it took to turn Parveen Baji's life around was a $70 loan from the Kashf Foundation. The illiterate mother of nine and wife of an abusive, drug-addicted husband,

Baji had resorted to asking neighbours for food. But the loan allowed her to start a jewellery business that quickly took off. Now she also owns a restaurant and catering business that employs eight people, and she is putting her children through high school and a son through college. 'Microfinance has changed my life,' she says.

8. Bernard McGraw, U.S.

After Hurricane Katrina, New Orleans native Bernard McGraw found himself homeless and unemployed. He settled his family in San Antonio, Texas and opened a Cajun restaurant in a shack in the city. When The Baptist University of the Americas asked him to set up shop on campus, he financed the project with a $4,265 loan from ACCION Texas-Louisiana to secure supplies and part-time employees. He now serves upwards of 100 customers a day and has done well enough to start 'Gumbo Under the Bridge', a programme to feed the homeless.

9. Likelesh Gebru, Europe

To supplement her husband's tiny income, Likelesh Gebru, a mother of five in Kacha Bira, started a small trading business. But when he was jailed for four years, Likelesh was left to provide for the family. As one of the first clients of the newly-built Wisdom Microfinance, she received 11 loans over ten years and her business grew exponentially. Her profits have allowed her, her children, and four of her relatives to go to school.

10. Bodour Al-Jayousi, Jordan

Bodour Al-Jayousi has had a difficult life. When her parents divorced she was forced to drop out of school at age 15 and help her father sell jewellery. The business took off after two loans from the Microfund For Women, but after a disagreement with her father she had to abandon the business. A third loan from MFW helped her buy the hair salon where she had found work but had earned just $350 per month. Today she employs up to 12 people and provides for her sister who is disabled.

2 January 2012

⇨ Information from OnlineMBA. Please visit www.onlinemba.com for further information.

What is the Cycle of Poverty?

Information from the Christian Reformed Church.

The Cycle of Poverty has been described as a phenomenon where poor families become trapped in poverty for generations. Because they have limited or no access to critical resources, such as education and financial services, subsequent generations are also impoverished.

Due to the many root causes of poverty and the complexity with how poverty is measured and defined, there are multiple Cycles of Poverty-based on, among other things, economic, social, spiritual and geographical factors. Many cycles overlap or perpetuate new cycles and therefore any attempt to depict the Cycle of Poverty will be far more simplistic than realistic.

The diagram opposite shows – in very simplistic terms – how a Cycle of Poverty related to hunger keeps a person or household poor in one of the world's developing countries.

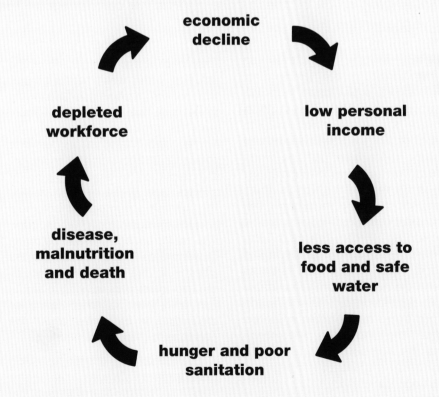

⇨ The above information is reprinted with kind permission from the Christian Reformed Church. Visit www.crcna.org for more information.

The seven myths of 'slums'

Conventional thinking on development issues is often characterised by many assumptions, clichés and rationalisations about the residents of slums. By challenging some of these core myths, we can focus on the causes of urban poverty, writes Adam Parsons.

For anyone who takes an interest in the problem of slums, a few basic facts will soon become clear. Firstly, global poverty is moving from rural areas to the cities. For the first time in human history, more than half the world population now lives in urban areas. Secondly, most of the world's urban population, most of its largest cities and most of its urban poverty is now located in Africa, Asia and Latin America – the so-called developing world. Thirdly, the growth in slums since the 1980s is both formidable and unprecedented (even though urban slums have existed in Europe since the Industrial Revolution), and the number of slum-dwellers worldwide is expected to increase in the decades ahead.

Beyond these facts, there seems to be little awareness about the reality of slums. Thanks to the tireless work of many activists and non-governmental organisations over many decades, the issue of global poverty is now high on the

international policy radar – but the issue of slums, which forms a major component of poverty in urbanising cities, still fails to register in most people's concerns. Much may be written about informal settlements in academic books and journals, but the depiction of slums in popular movies and literature also serves to reinforce a number of long-held prejudices against the urban poor. The indifference expressed by many governments and middle-class citizens to the struggles faced by the millions of people living in slums can also lead to other forms of discrimination or 'myths' about the solutions to inadequate housing.

Conventional thinking on development issues in the West is often characterised by many assumptions, clichés and rationalisations about the very poor who live in distant countries. In challenging some of these core myths, we are able to move beyond a response to poverty motivated by guilt or fear, and instead focus on the

structural causes of powerlessness that result in insecurity and deprivation. The following 'myths' about slums aim to give a general perspective on a range of key issues related to human settlements – including the impact of economic globalisation, the role of national governments, the significance of the informal sector of employment, the question of international aid, and the (little mentioned) controversy surrounding global slum data and development targets.

Myth 1: There are too many people

It is easy to believe that urban slums are a consequence of too many people living in cities, or too many poor people migrating from rural to urban areas for governments to contend with the strain on housing. But the real problem is rooted in outdated institutional structures, inappropriate legal systems, incompetent national and local governance, and short-sighted

urban development policies. From a wider perspective, the resurgence of a non-interventionist ideology in recent decades has weakened the role of national governments, and de-prioritised the importance of the state in planning for a more equitable distribution of resources in cities. Crippled by debt, forced to prioritise loan repayments over basic services such as healthcare, and held in thrall to the so-called Washington Consensus policies that demanded a withdrawal of government from almost every sphere of public life, it has been impossible for initiatives by the state or international agencies to keep pace with the rate of urban slum formation since the 1980s. In the simplest terms, the existence of slums is not an inevitable consequence of overpopulation, but a result of the failure of policy at all levels – global, national and local – and the adoption of an international development paradigm that fails to prioritise the basic needs of the poor.

Myth 2: The poor are to blame

Many people continue to blame the poor for their conditions of poverty. According to this deep-seated myth, the people who live in slums are antisocial, uneducated and unwilling to work, or else they would not be living in such conditions of squalor. In contrast to such popular prejudices, however, anthropologists and development practitioners have long observed that the poor are not a burden upon the urbanising city, but are often its most dynamic resource. While achieving considerable feats of inventiveness in self-help housing on an individual basis, the collective power of urban poor groups has produced exceptional results in building new homes and upgrading existing slum housing – as reflected in official development literature which recommends 'participatory slum improvement' as the best practice for housing interventions in developing countries. Yet for every example of a successful community-led upgrading scheme, there are as many examples of slum clearance operations and forced evictions. This constitutes one of the most crucial questions in the fight against urban poverty: will governments together recognise and support the ability of the poor to organise and help develop an inclusive city, or will they continue to view slum-dwellers as being 'anti-progress' and a threat to established institutions?

Myth 3: Slums are places of crime, violence and social degradation

A long-standing prejudice against the urban poor is the widespread view of slums as places of social degradation and despair, and of slum-dwellers as perpetrators of violence and crime. Although high levels of crime may occur in many informal settlements in developing countries, the popular depiction of life in slums often fails to acknowledge the deeper causes of insecurity and violence – including the links between levels of crime and incidences of poverty, inequality, social exclusion, and youth unemployment. These causal factors often go unacknowledged in films and media reports about slums. Many squatter settlements in the Southern Hemisphere also exhibit a communal solidarity that contradicts these negative stereotypes, along with innumerable examples of self-sacrifice, altruism and community service that serve as a laudable example for mainstream society. This is not to glorify or sentimentalise the urban poor and their self-help housing, as many slums can be equally characterised by the opposite qualities of ruthless individualism and petty-exploitation. But too often the stereotypical view of squatters as something 'other' – whether it be criminals, idlers, parasites, usurpers, prostitutes, the diseased, drunks or drug addicts – is the most common and misguided response to those who live in poor urban communities.

Myth 4: Slums are an inevitable stage of development

There is an underlying assumption to much of the debate surrounding slums and urban poverty: that the poor will get to our standard of living eventually, just so long as they follow our prescribed free market approach to development. Yet the policies for industrial growth followed by developed countries were not based on a *laissez-faire* ideology of free trade and state non-intervention, but instead used protectionist strategies for key industries in the earlier phases of development – which calls into question the neoliberal policy recommendations made to developing countries since the 1970s. The mainstream 'science' of economics is also based on the assumption that perpetual growth is the foundation of progress, even if common experience raises doubts about the environmental and social side-effects of unfettered capitalism. Furthermore, we can ask if it is acceptable to consider the appalling conditions and human abuses that defined cities all over Europe during the 19th century as an inevitable, even if disagreeable, part of progress in a rapidly industrialising city like Mumbai or Chang Hai. If not, our only choice is to consider alternative goals and more holistic models of development that prioritise social objectives ahead of the profit imperative and GDP, with a more equitable distribution of resources on the national and global level.

Myth 5: The free market can end slums

Many proponents of economic globalisation maintain a rigid faith in the power of market forces to end slums. Get the inefficient government out of the way, remains the assumption, and the beneficent power of the market mechanism and private capital will act as the levers of economic growth and widespread affluence. But after several decades of relying on the market as a cure-all for the ills of the 21st century, the increasing number of urban residents living in slums is sufficient evidence that the 'growth-first' strategy for development isn't sustainable. Employing market forces as the arbiter of resource distribution

is socially exclusive, not inclusive, and it does not function when there is a need to produce certain types of goods or services such as housing for the poor or welfare services for low-income groups. The deregulation and privatisation of public services also serves to directly undermine social welfare provision, and further compromises the ability of public agencies to meet the needs of those who cannot afford the market price for housing, healthcare, education and sanitation. In short, the efficiency-oriented, growth-led and internationally competitive strategies of the 'world class city' have failed to combat the problem of slums, and are more likely to exacerbate urban poverty than act as a solution in the future.

Myth 6: International aid is the answer

There may be more aid projects for improving the living conditions of the urban poor than ever before, but the current system of donor assistance has clearly failed to stem the tide of growing slum formation. The first problem is simply one of scale; urban poverty reduction is one of the lowest priorities for aid donations from most multilateral agencies and wealthy countries. A greater problem is the difference between the kind of assistance that is needed to ameliorate slums and the forms of action that are currently provided by international aid institutions. In particular, most official development assistance agencies have failed to develop relationships with slum residents and their representative organisations, and rarely assign any role to urban poor groups in the design and implementation of aid programmes. The priorities of aid agencies and development banks are also unlikely to favour the kind of redistributive policies that are central for giving the poor local control over the housing process. Although additional financial resources are imperative for upgrading slums in developing countries, it is doubtful that aid can successfully address the crisis in urban housing unless there is a transformation of the goals and priorities of the major donor countries and the institutions that govern the global economy.

Myth 7: There will always be slums

Few writers on urban development issues imagine a 'world without slums' in the future. In the polarised debates on urban poverty, both the 'slums of hope' and 'slums of despair' viewpoints tacitly accept the continued existence of slums. Part of the problem is one of semantics, as it is difficult to conceive of an end to 'slums' when the language used to describe them is limited and generalised. The UN's Millennium Development Goal on slums – to 'significantly improve the lives of 100 million slum-dwellers by 2020' – also implicitly accepts the existence of slums as an enduring reality, as achieving this (unacceptably low) target would hardly result in cities without slums. If urbanisation trends and cities are to become socially inclusive and sustainable, the development model that sustains them must be wholly reformed and reimagined. In the widest sense, a world without slums and urban poverty cannot be realised without a transformation of our existing political, economic and social structures. A first step lies in recognising the possibility of achieving a new vision of human progress based upon a fundamental reordering of global priorities – beginning with the immediate securing of universal basic needs. Only then can the twin goals enshrined in the Habitat Agenda of 1996 be translated into a concrete programme of action: 'adequate shelter for all' and 'sustainable human settlements development in an urbanising world'. The hope not only rests with the mobilisation of sufficient power through political organisation in the South, but also with the willingness of those in affluent societies to join voices with the poor, to sense the urgency for justice and participation, and to strengthen the global movement for a fairer distribution of the world's resources.

December 2010

⇨ The above information is reprinted with kind permission from Share The World's Resources. Please visit their website www.stwr.org/megaslumming/ for more information.

© Share The World's Resources

The biggest country you've never heard of

Bet you a quid you can't name this country.

It's more than twice the size of the UK and is home to over four million people.

Chances are, you're down a pound. That might not sound like much, but more than half of its population live on less than that for a whole day.

The Central African Republic is one of the poorest countries in the world. It has one of the lowest life expectancies (47 years) and highest child mortality rates (more than one in six kids die before their fifth birthday).

It hardly ever makes it onto the news and it has been largely ignored or forgotten by the international community. Away from our TV screens and newspapers, the young people of the Central African Republic have the grace to die quietly.

Its classrooms are empty, its hospitals destroyed, and its people are hungry. Many have fled their homes. The UN described the situation in Central African Republic as 'the world's most silent crisis'.

The Government is pretty ineffective beyond the capital Bangui, and armed violence is rife throughout the country. The Lord's Resistance Army terrorise people in the south – close to the porous borders with Congo and southern Sudan. There's an ongoing conflict between rival rebel groups and with the Government in the north.

It is surrounded on all sides by fellow 'Failed states': Democratic Republic of Congo, The Republic of Congo, Cameroon, Chad and Sudan.

So why have so few of us heard of it? It's hard to say. The answer could be one or all of these:

⇨ It's a very remote and insecure country – it's hard for tourists, journalists and NGO workers to travel around.

⇨ It's never had a famous (or infamous) citizen. No Premier League footballers, Presidents, musicians. Nothing.

⇨ The wars in neighbouring countries have perhaps been more bloody and have attracted more international attention.

Non-Government Organisations don't work there much, so you never see them talking about it in their appeals. It's a hard place to get funding for because it's not on government/UN/donor priority lists either. That's maybe because it isn't very politically significant because it doesn't export or trade much.

There's no oil or valuable mineral resources that have attracted the interest of multi-national companies, foreign governments and warlords.

Visit War Child's website www.warchild.org.uk to read about their project in Central African Republic.

⇨ Information from War Child. Visit www.warchild.org.uk for further information.

© War Child

Key Facts

⇨ The number of working-age childless adults [in the UK] in poverty is set to rise over 40% from its current level of 3.4 million to 4.9million by 2020. (page 4)

⇨ The most commonly used threshold of low income is a household income that is 60% or less of the average (median) British household income of that year ... In 2008/09, 13 million people in the UK were living in households below this low-income threshold. (page 5)

⇨ Around a third of all disabled adults aged 25 to retirements are living in low-income households. (page 5)

⇨ In 2010, the unemployment rate amongst young adults aged 16 to 24 was 25%. This proportion has been rising since 2004, when it was 12%. (page 6)

⇨ One in ten 16- to 18-year-olds are not in education, employment or training. (page 6)

⇨ Adults in the poorest fifth of the income distribution are much more likely to be at risk of developing a mental illness as those on average incomes. (page 7)

⇨ A third of homes in England were classified as non-decent in 2008. (page 7)

⇨ Two-fifths of people from ethnic minorities live in low-income households, twice the rate for white people. (page 7)

⇨ The report *Living on a Low Income in Later Life*, and a subsequent ICM poll, have shown nearly one in ten (9%) older people admit to be either 'finding it difficult' or 'really struggling' to manage their income. An estimated 4.5 million (33%) can only just afford to buy the basics. (page 8)

⇨ Research by Consumer Focus last year showed the number of payday loan users rose from 300,000 in 2006 to 1.2 million in 2009. (page 11)

⇨ Nine out of ten of the poorest communities – five of them in Liverpool – are in the north west of England with the 10th in Middlesbrough in the north eat, found by the Church Urban Fund (CUF). (page 12)

⇨ In the UK over 13 million people live in poverty. That's one in five who have to choose between switching on the heating or buying enough food to put a meal on the table. (page 13)

⇨ The UN has estimated that between 47 and 84 million more people have either remained extremely poor or been forced into poverty by economic downturn. (page 14)

⇨ The vast majority (84%) of the UK's least energy efficient homes could be brought up to near-average standards for less than £3,000. (This would bring them up to band E. The average for homes in the UK is now band D). (page 16)

⇨ In-work poverty was a growing phenomenon in the UK – the latest estimate is that 53 per cent of working age households in poverty have at least one working adult. This is around 2.3m households, after factoring in housing costs. (page 17)

⇨ The proportion of children living in poverty grew from one in ten in 1979 to one in three in 1998. Today, 30 per cent of children in Britain are living in poverty. (page 18)

⇨ Wealthier pupils perform better at all stages of schooling than pupils eligible for free school meals, regardless of race or gender. (page 21)

⇨ The international line of $1.25 a day is the average of the national poverty lines in the poorest 10–20 countries. (page 23)

⇨ By 2015, the number of people in developing countries living on less that $1.25 a day is projected to fall below 900 million. (page 25)

⇨ According to the International Labour Organization, one in five workers and their families worldwide were living in extreme poverty (on less than $1.25 per person per day) in 2009. (page 26)

⇨ On average four out of five refugees are hosted by developing countries. Afghans and Iraqis continue to be the largest refugee populations under the UNHCR mandate with three million and 1.7 million refugees, respectively, at the end of 2010. (page 27)

Absolute poverty

Inability to meet even the most basic survival needs. This includes life necessities such as food, water, shelter, clothing and health care.

Affluence

Wealth; abundance of money or valuable resources.

Benefits

We use the term 'state benefits' to describe any money that is given to us by the government. Benefits are paid to any member of the public, who may need extra money to help them meet the costs of everyday living.

Developing country

Also known as a less-developed county (LDC), a developing country is a nation with a low quality of life and poor standard of living. The UN has come up with the Human Development Index which measures the development of a country by looking at rates of literacy, life expectancy, gross domestic product, etc. In LDCs these all tend to be lower in comparison to other countries. Countries such as Ethiopia and Afghanistan are considered developing countries.

Developed country

Also known as a more developed country (MDC), a developed country has an advanced economy relative to other countries. In contrast with a developing country, MDCs tend to have higher rates of literacy, life expectancy and gross domestic product. Countries such as Germany and the United States are considered developed countries.

Microfinance

Providing loans, savings and other basic financial services to low-income individuals. This tends to involve smaller amounts of money than what a bank would traditionally provide. Many feel that access to microfinance will help lift poor people out of poverty, but it should not be viewed as the only tool to end it.

Millennium Development Goal

In 2000, world leaders decided that they needed a strategy to tackle poverty. They set and agreed targets, which are called the Millennium Development Goals. Goal 1 aims to eradicate extreme poverty and hunger, with a target of halving 1990 levels of poverty and hunger by 2015.

Non-Governmental Organisation (NGO)

This abbreviation stands for non-governmental organisation. This refers to an organisation that operates independently and are not part of any government. They usually serve a wider social aim, that may have political aspects, and are primarily concerned with promoting a cause or helping with development projects. Oxfam and Red Cross are examples of NGOs.

Poverty

Peter Townsend offers this definition of poverty: 'Individuals, families and groups in the population can be said to be in poverty when they lack the resources to obtain the types of diet, participate in the activities, and have the living conditions and amenities which are customary, or are at least widely encouraged and approved, in the societies in which they belong.'

Poverty line

The poverty line is the income level below which an individual can be said to be living in poverty. In the UK, the poverty line is define as 60 per cent of median household income, adjusted for household composition. Globally speaking, people defined as living in absolute poverty if they have less than $1 (USD) a day to live on.

Recession

When economic activities experience a significant decline, which in turn has a negative impact on things such as income, employment, industrial production and wholesale-retail sales. In the UK, a recession is defined as 2 successive business quarters, or 6 months, of negative growth.

Relative poverty

A measure of income inequality: dependent on social context, the standard of resources which is seen as socially acceptable in comparison with others in society. This differs between countries and over time. An income-related example would be living on less than X% of the average UK income.

Social exclusion

A lack of access to resources, possessions and activities which most members of society take for granted, thereby affecting on individual's quality of life.

Payday loan

A small, short-term loan which is intended to cover the lender's expenses until they receive their next paycheck (typically two weeks or less and for a sum of money ranging from $100 to $500). This is also referred to as a paycheck advance. This unsecured type of loan means the risk to the borrower is great due to the high rates of interest. Companies such as QuickQuid, Check'n Go, Wonga, etc provide this service.

Welfare reform bill

An Act of Parliament that changes the law relating to social security benefits. It aims to make the benefit system fairer and better able to tackle poverty, worklessness and welfare dependency (through things such as promoting work and personal responsibility).

Assignments

1. Using the website www.localgiving.com research a local charity or community project in your area. Using this information, create a leaflet that presents information about your chosen organisation and explains to your classmates how they can get involved with charitable projects in your area.

2. Design a series of 30-second television advertisements aimed at raising public awareness of global poverty. Use the information presented in Chapter 2, 'Global poverty', to aid you in drawing up a storyboard that informs the public about the implications of poverty.

3. Devise a TV chat show with your classmates in order to discuss poverty in the UK. One pupil will play the role of an individual who struggles with relative poverty, another pupil will play a person who lives an affluent lifestyle and does not partake in charitable activities, and another will play a government minister who will discuss how government legislation tackles UK poverty. Other classmates will be the audience and will have the chance to ask questions to the interviewees. The audience should consider how each 'character' relates to the others, and potentially has an impact upon them, and how poverty affects the different characters in various ways.

4. Use Chapter 1, 'Poverty in the UK', and the Internet to research issues regarding poverty in the UK. You should look at the impact of the recession upon families, along with issues regarding child poverty, statistics for national average income, along with health and housing issues. What are the main problems for UK citizens who are affected by poverty, and how can these issues be alleviated? Write a report discussing your findings.

5. Design a Power Point presentation that will demonstrate what you have learnt about poverty, both in the UK and around the world. Consider the reasons why it is important to educate children and young adults about the implications of poverty, and what can be done to help those in need.

6. Watch the 6 o'clock news on your preferred channel and, using their format, create a news report that informs viewers about the Central African Republic and the difficulties its citizens experience. Use the article 'The biggest country you've never heard of' on page 39 alongside the Internet to help you research further.

7. In small groups, brainstorm about the meaning of the term 'poverty' and the impact it has upon people's lives. Make notes on your discussion and feedback to the rest of the class.

8. Conduct a survey asking your classmates and parents about their perception of UK poverty and how they feel poverty impacts upon their lives, if at all. Using the statistics from this survey draw conclusions about poverty's impact in your area and detail the main concerns which you have discovered.

9. Using the article 'Key facts about poverty' on pages 5 to 8, draw up a weekly budget for a family of two adults and two children who are living in poverty. Work out how much money this family would spend on essential items such as food, transport, electricity and gas bills, then consider how much they would have left over for non-essential items such as entertainment.

10. Using the information provided in 'Food poverty on the rise as recession hits home' (page 17) and '2 skint 4 school' (page 21) script a monologue from the point of view of a twelve-year-old living in poverty in the UK. Discuss the impact of poverty upon you and your family. Explain the impact it has had upon your health, happiness, education and family lifestyle and consider how you might get out of poverty when you are older. What lifestyle decisions would you make?

11. Go onto 'Sport Relief's' website, www.sportrelief. com, and look at the Sport Relief campaign for 2012. Write a review on what issues the charity focuses on, and how the organisation interacts with local communities in order to assist citizens who may be suffering with poverty and the implications that it brings. In your opinion how successful has the organization been in achieving their goals?

12. Imagine that you represent a UK charity and compose a series of tweets which must be no more than 140 characters in length. The tweets should act as a series of hard-hitting messages which inform people about the effects of poverty in the UK and promote local community projects. You may also post links to external websites and photos which provide other information if you think this is helpful.

13. Look at the UN's *population of undernourished people* map on page 27. Choose a country with a very high percentage of undernourished citizens and use the Internet to conduct further research. Write a report examining the living conditions in your chosen country and highlight any charities or organisations that are working to help combat poverty in that area. Present the key findings of your report to your class.

Acknowledgements

The publisher is grateful for permission to reproduce the following material.

While every care has been taken to trace and acknowledge copyright, the publisher tenders its apology for any accidental infringement or where copyright has proved untraceable. The publisher would be pleased to come to a suitable arrangement in any such case with the rightful owner.

Chapter One: Poverty in the UK

What is poverty?, © Economic and Social research Council, *Relative poverty, absolute poverty and social exclusion*, © Guy Palmer, *UK poverty levels set to rise*, © Joseph Rowntree Foundation, *Key facts about poverty*, © Loughborough University, *The Welfare Reform Bill is the biggest benefits shake-up in 60 years*, © Guardian News & Media Ltd 2012, *The impact of the current Government's reforms on poverty*, © Institute for Fiscal Studies, *UK: Struggling families face astronomical interest on loans*, © 1998–2012 World Socialist Web Site, *Charity condemns 'unequal' England*, © 2012 The Press Association. All rights reserved, *Robin Hood Tax*, © 2010 The Robin Hood Tax, *What is fuel poverty?*, © National Children's Bureau, *Food poverty on the rise as recession hits home*, © Channel 4 2012, *Why end child poverty?*, © CPAG 2000–2012, *Child Poverty Strategy*, © Crown copyright 2012, *Barnardo's Child Poverty Quiz*, © Barnardo's 2012, *2 skint 4 school*, © CPAG 2000–2012.

Chapter Two: Global poverty

Poverty, © 2012 The World Bank Group, *Regional highlights*, © 2012 The World Bank Group, *Eradicating extreme poverty and hunger*, © United Nations, 2011, *The new 'bottom billion'*, © Bond 2012, *How 28 countries escaped the poverty trap*, © Guardian News & Media Ltd 2012, *Debate report: Britain must cut its overseas aid budget now*, © 2012 The Spectator (1828) Ltd, *Definitions of aid*, © World Poverty, *Britain to kick start banking for the poorest*, © Crown copyright 2012, *Ten amazing microfinance success stories*, © OnlineMBA 2012, *What is the Cycle of Poverty?*, © 1996–2012, Christian Reformed Church in North America, *The seven myths of 'slums'*, © Share The World's Resources, *The biggest country you've never heard of*, © War Child.

Illustrations:

Pages 9 and 18: Don Hatcher; pages 11 and 34: Simon Kneebone; pages 17 and 31: Angelo Madrid.

Images:

Cover, pages i, 36 and 37: © luoman; page 10: © liz hiers; pages 13, 14, 15: © Marmit; page 21: © Piotr Lewandowski; page 25: © Jon Ng; page 33: © Robert Stansfield/Department for International Development

Additional acknowledgements:

Editorial on behalf of Independence Educational Publishers by Cara Acred.

With thanks to the Independence team: Mary Chapman, Sandra Dennis, Christina Hughes, Jackie Staines, Jan Sunderland and Amy Watson.

Cara Acred

Cambridge

September, 2012